LAST-WICKET
STAND

LAST-WICKET
STAND

Searching for redemption, revival and a reason
to persevere in English county cricket

RICHARD CLARKE

First published by Pitch Publishing, 2020

Pitch Publishing
A2 Yeoman Gate
Yeoman Way
Worthing
Sussex
BN13 3QZ
www.pitchpublishing.co.uk
info@pitchpublishing.co.uk

A CIP catalogue record is available for this book
from the British Library.

ISBN 978 1 78531 721 7

Typesetting and origination by Pitch Publishing
Printed and bound in India by Replika Press Pvt. Ltd.

Contents

For DW Clarke (c)
and WS Clarke (+)

Foreword by
Ryan ten Doeschate

THE 2019 cricket season will live with me forever. Captaining Essex to the County Championship title and being a part of the side that won the Vitality Blast competition for the first time was a dream come true. After so many failures at the knockout phase, we were desperate to get our hands on the latter trophy. Meanwhile, for our medium- to long-term vision, it was critical to win the Championship again so quickly after 2017. It reaffirmed our ambition to be a fixture in Division One and to be a club that puts a big emphasis on four-day cricket.

It is important to remember these successes but, deep down, we all know that 'life is change'. We are all in perpetual transformation, either consciously moving towards a new self or subconsciously shifting with the times and circumstance. As I approached 40, I started to notice journalists increasingly wanted me to reflect and look back on my career. I'm not ready to sum it all up yet. However, these requests have forced me to take a step back and finally put some proper thought into assessing the gifts the cricketing gods have showered on me. It is surreal to look back on my own transformation. In the summer of 2003, I was in South Africa, had just graduated from university and was half-heartedly applying myself to a career in finance and accounting. I was still clinging on to the smallest hope that I would get a break in cricket but, to be honest, I was starting to feel I had missed the last train for that particular life. Then came my 'sliding doors' moment. I had been away on a golf weekend and was about to fly out to Holland to play club cricket and pursue a career in 'something finance-related'. But, after some convincing, I reluctantly agreed to play for a representative team against Essex at Newlands. At the time, I was not much more than a steady club cricketer, but Graham Gooch spotted something. My journey had begun. I would go on to have the honour of captaining Essex CCC and help to recreate some of the historic heights that the club had enjoyed 'back in the day'.

While this book is about cricket, it is also about redefining yourself. On a professional level, I am adjusting to stepping down from the captaincy in the winter of 2019, and from being an all-rounder to a batter and a very part-time bowler. To be honest, this is child's play for me. Remember, Essex had signed me as a medium-pacer back in 2003. It did not take too long to figure out that I would not cut it as a bowler. Still, I am also dealing with the fact that I am in the twilight years of my career; my very own last-wicket stand if you like. I have a group of young batters who are ready (or very close to ready) to take my spot. Then there is a major personal change. I became a dad for the first time at the end of 2019, so my life away from the cricket pitch has altered dramatically too. Passing on the captaincy and the timing of my impending fatherhood was entirely coincidental. My desire to step down was mainly influenced by the team's natural progression to a new identity of its own. This metamorphosis always transcends the individual.

Cricket, and more specifically county cricket, is continually evolving too. Right now, the sport is approaching a watershed moment; even an existential crisis in the eyes of some. The Hundred is an attempt to grow the sport and, most importantly, its coffers. It is pitched to attract new audiences and recycle the proceeds back into all levels of the game. As a player, I understand the desire for a new competition but even its staunchest supporters must acknowledge the potential downside for those counties who have been excluded from hosting a franchise.

Personally, I believe this new direction does not need to be seen as a zero-sum game and will not end up that way. But that means at the very least, as much effort should be directed to ensure that this progress does not work to the detriment of the established structure. Paraphrasing Sir Isaac Newton, to improve the future, one stands on the shoulders of giants. If county cricket is not the proverbial giant, it is the pillared legs that have supported and sustained the game in this country for well over a hundred years. Much of that strength has come from the very people who have championed the established first-class game. Let's not forget them.

It is vital that players care and recognise their positions as short-term custodians of the game and the clubs they represent. There is an obligation to the loyal fans and the history of the individual counties. A mercenary approach is morally wrong and an attack on the very integrity of the game. The myriad of new global tournaments can detract from a player's attachment to 'their team'. A modern-day cricketer can easily play for seven different sides in a year. But there is scope for travelling the world, fulfilling short-term contracts and maintaining genuine care for the teams and communities you represent. I tried really hard to reinvigorate that sort of passion at Essex and the players were fantastic at buying in. We could not have had two better head coaches in Chris Silverwood and Anthony McGrath to lead this change. I do not think it's a coincidence that they are both Yorkshiremen. The purpose, the search for meaning, the reason for caring and committing is complex and I've always thought it a chicken and egg scenario – winning teams are happy rather than happy teams are winners.

Despite all this, many fear that the County Championship format is at risk of losing its relevance and may suffer a slow death. While this may be considered alarmist, many have mooted at least a partial demise via the loss of some of our counties. I am a huge fan of county cricket and would be bitterly disappointed to see it phased out. It has no peers in domestic first-class competition around the world and still enjoys a decent following. The shorter formats are more exciting and, as attendance figures show, blatantly more popular. But, for players, I truly believe that the Championship is still the most coveted title in the domestic game.

Being fortunate enough to have won two titles with Essex, I know just how tough and strenuous it can be at the top of Division One. Draws have become a rarity and nine wins seems to be the new magic formula for lifting the Championship. This does not leave much room for slip-ups. From July till the end of the 2019 season, we knew we could only afford one or two poor days if we wanted to keep our title challenge alive. The elation and satisfaction that this produced exceeds anything I have experienced in playing cricket around the world.

Championship cricket is the breeding ground of the England Test team. While not necessarily top of our weekly 'to do' list, one of the goals of any county is to produce players for their country. Essex have a rich history of producing Test players with Graham Gooch, Keith Fletcher, Nasser Hussain and Alastair Cook amongst England's finest. It was a truly proud moment for everyone at the club when Tom Westley graduated out of the Essex team and into the Test arena in 2017.

The county game will remain important to the ECB while the five-day international game is popular. The appetite for Test cricket varies greatly across participating nations but the game is trying to move with the times. Its recent transformation means you rarely see a dull day now, let alone a whole Test or entire series. Despite a 'quick-hit' culture and endless entertainment options, thankfully it retains an especially strong following in the UK. The 2019 Ashes could hardly have demonstrated this any more clearly.

But away from the Test team conveyor belt, the financial numbers and even the playing side, county cricket still has so much to admire. The format lends itself to an intimate personal connection. You see familiar faces, you have the time to stop for a quick chat, there is far more downtime in play to observe and absorb what is going on behind the advertising boards. At a non-Test playing venue like Chelmsford, there's a unique internal connection with the non-playing staff. In sporting parlance, it is a family club. One of the hallmarks of the 2017 title was that it felt more like a triumph for the club than just the team. This connection is extended to the wider community, albeit to a lesser degree. As players, we try to be aware of what we are giving to our loyal supporters, and while a satisfying scoreboard cannot always be guaranteed, effort and commitment should never be questioned. The insight from the stories in this book, the musings of a passionate and caring supporter, gives food for thought to someone who has had the privilege of being inside the field of play and only goes to strengthen the affection for, and the responsibility to, the fans of our game.

For as long as I have known him, Rich Clarke has been a fiery yet quiet advocate of the club and county cricket in general. I can attest to his passion for Essex CCC; it's not unusual to see him pop up on the third morning of a match somewhere many miles away from home. We both support Arsenal and have spent a fair amount of time chatting about both football and cricket over the years. Having worked at Arsenal, and close to the action at that, Rich knows and understands the mechanics of the most revered league in the world, and with that the dangers at the highest end of commercialised sport. His extensive experience across codes and continents puts him in the perfect place to assess the state of county cricket. In this book, he parallels his life's landmarks and major milestones with county cricket's arrival at an equally important juncture in its own existence. He manages to intertwine and compare some of these personal struggles and challenges, such as turning 50, with the difficulties faced by the sport he so loves.

We all have to be honest, many of the arguments for maintaining the existing structure of county cricket are based on sentiment. Even an arch advocate such as Rich attests to that. But sentiment is the currency of romantics and fools in the increasingly commercially driven sports world. County cricket will have to transform itself to stay relevant. It will need to sustain a level of competence and professionalism that can keep feeding and strengthening the national team. The suggestion that the number of first-class teams will eventually be reduced seems plausible and dare I say even sensible. Obviously, Essex are one of the non-Test hosting counties and would appear to be in danger of facing the chop if a reduced roster is pursued. As a result, there is an even greater need to be a competitive first-class team on the pitch – it may be a deciding factor in our very existence. The same is true for all the other non-Test counties. There is time for both individual club and county cricket itself to transform and adapt. To remain relevant, it must react to change and evolve into something that is purposeful beyond the sheer delight it brings to so many.

Essex are a proud club and we will continue to improve. It is more than an appetite just to sustain our recent success – we are willing to lick the plate too. It is this type of an attitude that will make county cricket and all its clubs indispensable in the years to come.

Here's to the future.

Introduction

THE WORLD was fighting off the threat of a virulent pandemic as this book was being completed. The UK was in lockdown and there appeared to be only one thing of which we could be certain, the country would emerge as a different place in its wake.

The previous five years had been dominated by the fractious factionalism of Brexit, with Leavers and Remainers fighting a long and bitter battle for the future of the UK. All that dissipated in the early months of 2020 as COVID-19 swept across the globe, taking down country after country. Now, the primary battle was to stay alive.

So we washed our hands, stayed at home, 'flattened the curve' and, above all, supported our National Health Service.

England cricketer Jack Leach likened the role of the public to his part in a doughty 76-run last-wicket stand with Ben Stokes that secured victory in the third Test at Headingley and kept alive the 2019 Ashes series. The Somerset tail-ender contributed just one run, a stolen single behind square to bring the scores level. Then

Stokes bashed the winning boundary to create one of the great cricketing moments of the summer. 'Being boring is boring guys!' he tweeted. 'But if it gets the job done it's definitely worth it! We are all batting at 11 so let's not get ahead of ourselves and start playing shots. Defend your stumps, one ball at a time and let Stokes do his thing.' Even in such trying, unprecedented times, the nuance and complexity of cricket had provided the perfect simile for life.

In comparison to this, my own last-wicket stand, and that of county cricket itself, suddenly seemed beyond trivial. By the time it is fully eradicated, COVID-19 will have caused hundreds of thousands of deaths and wrecked millions of lives. The global economy is expected to take its hardest hit in a century; this will mean people lose their jobs and many will face poverty. In contrast to such hardship, sport is inconsequential and highlighting the supposed problems of one comfortably-off individual is frankly pathetic.

You know this, I know this but then, deep down, we always did. Those of us with an intrinsic love of cricket, football or any other sport always understood it mattered for nothing, even if it paid our mortgage. Yet what was the reaction when someone would tell us 'it was only a game'? One of the few silver linings of the strange period under lockdown in 2020 is the potential for a recalibration of our priorities. From rediscovering the importance of the NHS and neighbourly support to an emphasis on physical fitness and mental health, in this period many of us resolved to do better and simply be better. We can only hope this is one permanent positive from a truly tragic time in our modern history.

The vast majority of this book was written well before anyone had heard of COVID-19. In the early months of 2019, my priorities were very different. On a personal front, everything appeared to be fine. Having returned from living abroad at the end of 2016, my family had settled into English life once more. My wife won the race between us to get a permanent job so I became a consultant and the primary carer of the family. I expected this to be a temporary situation. I had always been able to command the higher salary plus I needed the structure and fulfilment of a career. Though my wife is extremely capable at her job, she was always struck by the nagging guilt of a working mother. There was no patriarchal plot in this. I was happy enough as a househusband for a while, she was happy enough as the breadwinner but our preferences were around the other way.

However, I had played my hand badly by leaving myself without permanent work as I approached my 50th birthday. Like many before me, I failed to see my own impending invisibility in middle age. At this point, it is important to proffer the first of many apologies that will follow in this book. There was so much for which I should be grateful, not least the family around me. However, the working world defined my identity, and it had always told me to compete and compare. In such circumstances, unless you are constantly winning, bitterness, anger and depression will eventually snare you. In that British way, I kept calm-ish and carried on but all three would become my captor to a greater or lesser extent.

Meanwhile, county cricket was having its own identity crisis. The Hundred was on the horizon. In 2020, for the first time since competitive cricket had started in England in the late 19th century, the first-class counties would not be the principal focus. Instead, eight city-based franchises were set to dominate the key period during the summer. Like many devotees of the four-day Championship format, I feared a hidden and potentially destructive agenda. I resolved to record this 'last summer'. So I followed my county, Essex CCC, throughout the campaign. From the genteel pre-season friendly at Fenner's, home of Cambridge University to a beer-soaked Vitality Blast Final at Edgbaston. I was there for the first ball of the Championship season and the winner-take-all final game at Taunton. I had followed Essex throughout my life and briefly worked for the club as a freelance journalist a decade or so earlier. Part of my brief had been to write a semi-serious, slightly historical, slightly morose column under the pseudonym of The Grumbler. After that ended, I retained the persona on social media.

Not that there was much to moan about at Essex since I had returned to the UK. Within weeks, the club had finally secured promotion to Division One and, in 2017, won its first County Championship title in a generation. As the next chapter explains, it was the perfect personal distraction at the time. Luckily for me, the 2019 campaign will go down as one of the best seasons in the club's history. It was fast turning into a golden era and an oasis of joy amid considerable personal turmoil. In my mind, it was proof once more that, though sport could not heal, it might just provide a Band-Aid of distraction while your soul repaired itself. The *Wisden Almanack* would devote a prominent article to this very topic in the 2020 edition. The triumph of the first great cricket team from Chelmsford was recorded in David Lemmon's wonderful book *Summer Of Success: The Triumph Of Essex CCC In 1979*. I poured over those pages as a child. This book endeavours to describe the stories and the numbers behind the games in a similar, if less detailed, fashion. While not reverting to scorecards, hopefully, you will find out who did what and when, with an estimation of how important it was at the time and a few amusing tales along the way. Essex and Somerset went toe-to-toe in the second half of the summer and I want you to feel every blow. In the Vitality Blast, you will understand how it felt in the stands as the trophy was decided from the final ball. There is no inside knowledge, every observation is my own or taken from publicly available media. If you want to know why Simon Harmer took all those wickets or how Sir Alastair Cook grinds out so many runs then these pages will provide a view, but it will be no better than yours. This is just one fan's story.

The origins of each entry were written in the stands with my laptop perched on my knees. I have developed and embellished them in retrospect but the essence and the emotion remains the same. However, Lemmon's book is from a very different time. My copy has a picture of an Essex CCC-clad teddy bear on the front; this one shows three maudlin men watch a game at Chelmsford under darkened skies. No one was asking such searching questions about the future of the County Championship 40 summers ago while Twenty20 and the term 'status anxiety' were yet to be invented.

If you only like the cricket tales then skip the personal side and please forgive my indulgences. It took a lot of courage to lay down my emotions for all to see. In fact, it was utterly against the grain. One of the reasons I feel at home watching County Championship games at Chelmsford is that nothing is asked of me. I can be a contented introvert. One of those silent, solitary older men who just sit there and watch. This book is about communicating how much the environment surrounding this game is loved, revered and important, even if it is not well attended.

The economics of domestic cricket have been hard to sustain for decades now. When the market for Test match rights appeared to soften, the England and Wales Cricket Board (ECB) knew they must act. One of the main reasons for playing 14 four-day games a season had been the conveyor belt of players it provided for the national team. Tests were still a 'cash-cow' and some of the proceeds went back to hold up the 18 first-class counties. Even the most ardent county fan with the rosiest of tints on their spectacles would accept change was required. However, the introduction of The Hundred reminded me of a toddler trying to force a large square brick into a smaller circular hole. It was bashed this way and that, from all sorts of angles when a simpler, more straightforward solution was close to hand. I have tried to reduce my ire to one somewhat emotional chapter written at the height of the debate but the questions its development has raised regarding county cricket pervade this book.

What is the point? Is it worth preserving in its current form? Are its values still relevant? What meaningful contribution can it make? Was it ever that good anyway? How much should it change? How much can it change? Should it just disappear quietly over the next few decades while we all simply move on?

But then, in the summer of 2019, I was asking precisely the same questions of myself.

2017 (and the worst of a wonderful season)

IT IS very possible that I will never get over 2017. From a cricketing perspective, it was the year when it all came right in such unexpected fashion. Supporters of any sports team learn to live in hope rather than expectation. Deep down, even the most sour-faced misanthrope in the stands always retains an inkling that this could be their year, that youngster might just come good or the old warhorse has one more victory left inside.

We fans have to believe this, we must. If reason and experience fully triumph in the fight for our expectations there would be no point in watching any sport, let alone one as derided and ignored as English domestic cricket. The context for this tale, both on the pitch at Chelmsford and inside my head, was moulded by the events of 2017. Let us deal with the cricket first.

While there was much to admire in the opening game with Lancashire at Chelmsford, no one would have labelled Essex champions-elect. Only a stoic, seven-hour 141 not out from Dan Lawrence stopped the visitors from claiming victory. This game saw the debut of South African-born spinner, Simon Harmer, who becomes a leading actor in this story. A little over two years later his exploits would see him lauded as the club's best ever overseas signing. Neil Wagner, an aggressive left-handed pace bowler from New Zealand with a liquid action, also made his Essex bow at Chelmsford. He would announce himself by taking six Somerset wickets in the second innings of the next Championship game at Taunton. That performance still left Essex chasing a daunting 255 batting last. However, Alastair Cook, available and batting for the first time since relinquishing the England captaincy, hit 110. By the time he was dismissed, the visitors were 39 runs from victory with wickets to spare.

That 19-point haul in the West Country was the first Division One victory by Essex since July 2010. They had been languishing in the second tier since then and only won promotion the previous season. That is why the season to follow seemed like a fairy-tale and, though the odds were far shorter and the financial disparity much greater, it can be talked about in the same breath as Leicester City's stunning Premier League triumph in 2015/16.

Ten Doeschate's team would be labelled Invincibles at the end of the season for remaining unbeaten throughout. Their doggedness and ability to turn around difficult positions was obvious from these early fixtures. However, only a huge stroke of luck kept a 0 under the letter L in the table after the game at Lord's at the end of April.

The top three Middlesex batsmen, Sam Robson, Nick Gubbins and Steve Eskinazi, all hit centuries as the home side declared on a daunting 507/7 and then dismissed Essex for 295. The weather forecast was poor yet home captain James Franklin eschewed the follow-on and used up 36 overs to add 239/3 in the second Middlesex innings. Essex were 19/0 overnight and I went along to Lord's on the last day sure of defeat, but I had not been to the home of cricket to see my team in a few years. Cricketing cathedrals such as Lord's are strange places on mundane afternoons in the County Championship. It is akin to visiting a historic battlefield, with echoes of the past around every corner. I picked out the place I sat as a child when Joel Garner extracted the middle stump with a throw from the boundary to enact a run-out against England. Later that afternoon when the Red Stripe had taken full effect, an ebullient West Indies fan would chastise the home supporters when they graciously stood for another Viv Richards half-century by snapping: 'Sit down, sit down, that is nothing more than we expect.'

Essex had seemed likely losers at Lord's since the end of day two. However, the batsmen dug in amid numerous stoppages. Even Ravi Bopara curtailed his natural stroke-making tendencies as he trudged to 32 off 93 deliveries in just over two hours. Finally, with 13 overs left and Essex 160/8, Wagner and Aaron Beard marched sharply off the pitch after the umpires declared bad light once again. The visitors went home with eight points and their unbeaten record intact. It was as close as they would come to defeat in the Championship all season.

Essex had not enjoyed consecutive campaigns in the top division since the County Championship split in two at the turn of the millennium. They had yo-yoed in the early years after the separation but then settled into the second division despite a host of finishes just outside the promotion places. In that context, most fans would have settled for a safe season – one point above the relegated teams might be enough. Until the end of May, the team had shown they had been hard to beat. A crucial quality, but Cook had been central to their solitary victory and he would be on England duty later in the campaign. The performance against Hampshire at Chelmsford was the first sign of the destructive qualities that would bring ten wins, twice the tally of anyone else that season.

On the first day, Nick Browne was dismissed from the fifth ball and Tom Westley was bowled by Kyle Abbott with four balls scheduled to go in the day. In between, the latter joined Cook in a 243-run partnership, the best for any wicket against Hampshire. Given that start, the Essex first innings score of 360 may have been a little disappointing. However, the bowlers would make it appear mountainous. Hampshire lost five wickets with the score on 18 and only an eighth-wicket partnership of 75 lifted them to 115 all out. Jamie Porter finished with stunning figures of 14-5-24-5.

This seemed to happen consistently throughout the 2017 campaign. The opposition would barely reach 20 before a couple of batsmen had returned to the pavilion and the crowd would not clap the half-century until they were four-down. Hampshire were 50/5 in the second innings following on and were beaten by an innings and 97 runs in two-and-a-half days. The win put Essex top of the table by a point from Surrey, who arrived at Chelmsford next. Again, the visitors lost early wickets on the opening day. This time Matt Quinn shared the scalps with Porter as the visitors slumped to 31/5 in the opening 50 minutes. However, Surrey would be 303/2 for the remainder of the day as an imperious Kumar

Sangakkara shared a stand of 191 with Sam Curran. For the Sri Lankan, it was his fifth hundred in successive innings. Only seven other people had achieved this in first-class cricket with just C.B. Fry, Mike Procter and Don Bradman adding a sixth. I was sat on the top deck of the Tom Pearce Stand when Sangakkara made history by reaching three figures. Everyone rose to their feet. When the 39-year-old doubled that tally, Cricinfo pointed out that there was no discontent, only appreciation. County cricket supporters understand greatness even if it happens to be making their team grovel. Apart from Curran's 90 and Stuart Meaker's late 49, there was precious little support for Sangakkara and a century from Lawrence saw Essex's 383 nudge them in front after both first innings were complete. Surrey seemed to be serenely playing out the day before Porter took 5-15 in 27 balls and soon after Westley took a return catch to dismiss Sangakkara 16 runs short of a sixth century, but the game would peter out.

The doughty Porter ended the game with figures of 9-160 and was already looking like a key contributor again. In 2014, he had told the *Brentwood Gazette*: 'To be honest, I had almost given up on ever playing the game professionally. Last year I was working in an office, just playing on a Saturday and it wasn't really working out. But this season has completely changed it around for me. I think just that change of attitude has really worked for me and given me the determination to do well.'

Porter was dismissed as too slow and 'not doing enough' for England recognition by the early judges and, as I write, despite two Championship medals on his mantelpiece, he has still not represented his country. A year or so later, he got into a minor Twitter spat with Kevin Pietersen during which the highly talented former England batsman remarked 'if playing for Essex is living the dream then f**k I have got it wrong'. Porter replied: 'Just because you look down on county cricket doesn't mean it doesn't mean a lot to the blokes playing it but [I] guess you don't see much past your own shadow.' Understandably, the Essex bowler would delete his message but it was a perfect riposte and, in a way, lies at the heart of this book. Perhaps the fact that Porter came close to calling time on his cricket career before it had really started made him appreciate it all the more. Certainly, after a shaky start, he has proved to be a very successful county cricketer. This is so much more than most of us ever achieve. Yes, it is less than Pietersen but surely the most important aspects of sport and life are about fulfilling 100 per cent of your potential and improving the environment for those around you. By that measure, Porter has been more successful than Pietersen, whose England's career was curtailed in its prime after continuing disruption and disagreement. I venture Sir Alastair Cook would probably admit he has less innate talent than the 2005 Ashes hero but he ended up scoring thousands more runs at Test level. Sports fans are often guilty of viewing talent in a vacuum. It is a fundamental misunderstanding to see the exploits of 'the gifted one' as not underpinned by sheer hard work, existing outside of a team environment and almost possessing a licence to agitate. Fans love a match-turner and eulogise over the mavericks but, deep down, they really appreciate consistency, commitment and longevity. Insanely talented though he may be, there is no part of a Test or county ground named after Kevin Pietersen but then that is probably not how he judges his achievements. Each to his own.

By the time Essex started their rapid return fixture against Surrey at Guildford they had lost top spot to Hampshire. But we were entering June and last year's Division Two champions could now be classed as real contenders for the top prize this time. Looking back, the fixture might have been a key moment. Not 'the' key moment but one of many tests the team passed in this incredible season. Mark Stoneman's 197 was the foundation of Surrey's 399 all out in the first innings. Essex were wobbling at 134/4 before Bopara and ten Doeschate added 120 for the fifth wicket. The Dutchman would finish unbeaten on 168, his highest Championship score for Essex at the time, as his team finished 435 all out. Harmer's 4-83 kept Surrey down to 288 in their second innings and, on a fast-scoring ground, Nick Browne (77) and Tom Westley (108*) shone as the visitors recorded an eight-wicket win. It looked straightforward in the record books but it was anything but and Essex had once again demonstrated a key virtue that season – different players stepping up at different times. The likes of Lawrence, Cook and Porter had already played key roles – this time it was ten Doeschate and Harmer. They had even overcome the loss of opening bowler Quinn, who was absent from the first day onwards with a back spasm. He would not play again that season because of a stress fracture but he, too, had made a contribution.

On the Friday before the game against Warwickshire began, Essex had endured an agonising last-over defeat in the semi-final of the Royal London One-Day Cup. A staggering 743 runs were scored in 99.3 overs in one of the greatest run-fests in domestic cricket history. The same square was used for the visit of the 'Bears' and Essex would hit 541/9 declared in their first innings, albeit at a slower rate. Browne carved out a sluggish but crucial 84 off 244 balls to set the foundation, then Ravi Bopara (192) and James Foster (121) shared a 229-run stand for the sixth wicket as the home side set up a daunting score. It was the former's first Championship century for almost three years and, for the latter, it represented a return to batting form after Adam Wheater had kept him out of the side early in the campaign. Upon reaching the milestone he leapt up and punched the air three times.

Foster is one of my favourite ever Essex players. I have a weakness for wicketkeepers and this one was highly skilled. He was selected for England A after just four appearances for his county and made his Test debut in India at the end of the following year. A broken arm, Alec Stewart and changes in selection policy meant Foster only won seven Test caps despite being hailed as the best keeper in the country. He finally won a Championship winners' medal in 2017 and would retire at the end of the following season. Looking back now, I wonder if Foster is content with what he achieved or bothered about what he did not? As you will find out, these are the questions that vexed me.

Harmer was starting to spin games the way of Essex. He took 6-92, his first Championship five-for, as Warwickshire were dismissed for 283 at Chelmsford and then 8-36 in the second innings as they mustered a mere 94 following on. Aggregate figures of 14-128 from 66 overs represented his career-best at the time. That sort of higher mathematics would become familiar in the years to come.

Essex had belief, momentum and a 14-point lead after seven games. They would start the second half of the

Championship season with the most incredible finish to a four-day game I have witnessed. The ECB's experiment in day/night cricket, complete with a rather controversial pink ball, seemed to be ending with a whimper. The weather had not helped. Evening cricket in the last days of June conjured up visions of Panama hats and Hawaiian shirts. On the day, I was dressed like a kind of Essex-themed Eskimo.

The home side had Middlesex by the scruff of the neck right from the start at 2pm on the first day. Wagner's replacement, Mohammad Amir, had Nick Gubbins lbw with his sixth ball for the club then Nick Compton was caught behind off Porter in the following over to leave Middlesex 2/2. Middle-order defiance saw them to 246 all out but Harmer spun out the tail, taking figures of 5-77 in the process. Cook and Browne would put the visitors' effort into context by amassing 106 without loss in the final 36 overs. At the dinnertime interval, if that is the correct label, Essex had honoured one of its finest servants by renaming their pavilion after Doug Insole. The all-rounder had played 450 first-class games and captained the county throughout the 1950s, taking them from bottom-feeders to title contenders. In 1955, he amassed a gargantuan 2,427 runs, including nine centuries. Those feats brought him an England recall, though his international career would consist of only nine caps. In fact, his post-playing cricket life would outshine his time in the middle, though Insole's tenure saw turbulent times. He was chairman of England selectors when Basil D'Oliveira was initially omitted from the touring side to South Africa in 1968/69 and during the 'Packer Circus' in the late 1970s. These moments loomed large in the obituaries published when he died little over a month later. But his service to Essex CCC was well known and widely regarded. It was entirely fitting that he should take in the applause of the Chelmsford crowd one more time before his passing.

Day two against Middlesex was washed out and rain was still in the air for much of the third. However, Browne and Cook continued their steady domination, putting on a total of 373 for the first wicket. This was a record opening stand, breezing past the 316 between Graham Gooch and Paul Prichard in 1994 and the best partnership for any wicket in a game between the counties. Middlesex got the first wicket of the day at 6.55pm when Cook was caught off Ollie Rayner. But the punishment did not stop as Varun Chopra blazed six sixes in a 75-ball century. He was only playing as Tom Westley had left for England Lions duty after the first two days. Browne's odyssey finally ended on 221 after 384 deliveries in just over eight and a half hours. The phrase 'Daddy Hundred' had always been associated with Graham Gooch. Renowned for his discipline and self-motivation, the opener would chastise himself for giving his wicket away at any time but especially when he had reached three figures and was 'set'. Cook's powers of concentration at the crease were almost legendary; reportedly he believed long sessions as a chorister at Bedford School set the foundations. But this was the third successive time Browne had turned a century into a double century. His first hundred had come from 240 deliveries and his second from 128. It was a day worth shivering in the stands to watch.

The final day was about survival for Middlesex, who were already fearing the drop after winning the title the previous season on the last afternoon against Yorkshire in front of 10,000 spectators at Lord's. The normally explosive Paul Stirling ground out 55 from 142 deliveries and opener Compton took up 381 minutes compiling an obdurate 120. There were just over 12 overs left in the day when he was lbw to Harmer playing no shot. Middlesex were six down and the South African had them all. I was hunched under an overcoat at the top of the Tom Pearce Stand and had started to contemplate leaving before Compton's dismissal. The 9pm close was rapidly approaching, it was cold, I had a long drive home and Middlesex seemed to have enough fight left in them.

With six overs left to bowl, Essex still needed four wickets and had seemingly set up camp around the batsmen. Play was condensed into a playing strip and an area two yards all the way around. There had been oohs, aahs and intensity but Middlesex were hanging on with grim determination. Then Harmer had Ryan Higgins caught at slip and, three balls later, trapped Rayner lbw. He had now taken all eight wickets in the Middlesex innings and, in that over, reignited the home side's belief. Dan Lawrence ruined that run but set up the victory by trapping Toby Roland-Jones in front. One more to go. Four balls into the penultimate over, Harmer rapped No 11 Steven Finn on the pads, the Essex players erupted and umpire David Millns raised his finger. There were less than 1,000 of us at Chelmsford that night, maybe only 500. Around me, on the top tier of a stand beside a cricket field in rural Essex, every middle-aged man jumped up, broke into smiles and seemed happy to engage with those around him. What else but sport could do that?

I recorded some video of the celebrations on my phone. Harmer raced off in the direction of the Felsted School

Stand pursued by his team-mates. Ten Doeschate broke away quickly to shake hands with the umpires and the two Middlesex batsmen, who adhering to cricket's important niceties, stayed in the middle to walk off together. I looked back at my recording in researching this passage; the time stamp read 8:57pm and 27 seconds. Harmer finished the innings with 9-95, the first nine-for by an Essex bowler since Mark Ilott's effort in 1995. He had taken 14-172 in the game and recorded 28-300 in the space of a week. Essex were now 29 points clear with eight of the 14 games played. The Championship was far from over but they were favourites, still unbeaten and, after this victory, an almost irresistible force.

My second-biggest regret of the 2017 season was not travelling to Yorkshire for the game at Scarborough. It is renowned as one of the most atmospheric, picturesque and traditional venues on the circuit and, being an outground, Essex only appear there periodically. A crowd of almost 6,000 saw Mohammad Amir sear through their batting line-up and leave the home side 74/9 at lunch. The Pakistani would finish with figures of 11.2-4-18-5 as Yorkshire were dismantled for 113. Essex were 188/8 themselves at the close thanks largely to ten Doeschate's cautious aggression but would add another 43 on the second morning. Then Mohammad Amir (5-54), ably assisted by Porter (4-41) saw Yorkshire dismissed for 150 on the stroke of tea. The visitors had completed victory inside two days. On top of the obvious ignominy, the early defeat was also a hefty blow to the coffers for this otherwise joyous festival.

It was the end of August and Essex were now 41 points clear, a difference that represented two solid defeats and they had the momentum of four straight wins. Surely

Somerset, mired in a relegation battle and lacking their two best bowlers, would put up little resistance? On a roasting Bank Holiday Monday morning, ten Doeschate won the toss and Chopra stroked successive boundaries in the first over. All seemed well in the world from an Essex perspective. An hour later they were 39/4 with the captain digging in to lift his team out of a deep, dark hole. However, the Dutchman would join Nick Browne (44) and Foster in the pavilion for the addition of just eight runs in the 90s. The final three wickets gleaned a crucial 51, with Mohammad Amir hitting five fours in an 18-ball 22. Still, 159 all out represented a poor return for a title-chasing team. However, yet again in a time of crisis, someone found stellar form.

Harmer had been taking most of the headlines but Porter had been consistently picking up wickets, a feat that had brought an England Lions call-up. In the last session of the first day against Somerset, the paceman took centre stage, picking up high-quality wickets in the form of Marcus Trescothick, Tom Abell and James Hildreth. Then Harmer and Mohammad Amir mopped up the tail at the start of day two, leaving Somerset with a lead of only five. At the close, in front of a crowd of 2,500 supporters, Essex had turned the game around. Eventually, they would leave Somerset chasing 289 for victory. Porter sliced through their top order then he and Harmer polished off the rest. The former took 7-55, taking his match figures to 12-95. The title was starting to look inevitable. However, the next game was at the home of the only side with any hope of catching them, Lancashire.

In stereotypical fashion, it rained. A lot. Five sessions were lost to the weather, including the entire first day.

Once play began, the most notable contributions were former England batsman Haseeb Hameed grinding out 88 from 250 balls and debutant Sam Cook bowling Liam Livingstone to collect his opening first-class wicket. The game effectively ended at 4.10pm on the final day with substitute Essex captain Varun Chopra declaring at 202/8 to prevent Lancashire picking up an extra bowling point. They got on the M6 with their lead still at a healthy 36 points.

By the time Essex went to Warwickshire for the penultimate game, the calculators were at the ready. The mathematics at Edgbaston and elsewhere could determine when the visitors would secure the title and if the home side were to go down. By now, Wagner had replaced Mohammad Amir as overseas bowler but it was Porter who reduced the home side to 12/2 after 15 deliveries. Ten Doeschate had claimed an uncontested toss to take advantage of early conditions as the start times had moved to 10.30am now it was September. His bowlers did the rest. Only Dominic Sibley's 76 saw Warwickshire squeeze past 200. Chopra's 98 set up the Essex response of 369/9 declared and suddenly we seemed to have a clear equation. Victory in Birmingham seemed assured and second-place Lancashire were struggling at Somerset. It was coming together; an Essex victory would all-but secure the club's first title in 25 years. A later lapse by Lancashire would make it mathematically certain.

This only dawned on me when I was a few pints deep at a 'networking night' that had actually started late in the afternoon in central London. It was held at a gentleman's club, by that I mean the type full of wood-panelled walls, high net-worth individuals and the tacit misogyny, not a strip joint. It sounds posher than it was and I was only there for the aforementioned networking, which for an introvert seems to be selling yourself to people you barely know in the hope of financial gain. To be honest, there seemed more morality and honesty in stripping. My abiding memory was paying over £30 for a single gin and tonic – that should tell you the story of the evening. However, I was looking for a job and there were some influential people in attendance. We all know the most important work at a conference is undertaken in the pub afterwards and it was there that I fully caught up with the equation facing Essex at Edgbaston the following day.

Unfortunately, in true 1990s sitcom fashion, I was g'wann-ed into a couple more pints than necessary before shambling my way around the tube network and back to my house. Forewarned of a heavy night, my wife took responsibility for the school run the next morning but I woke up early enough to mull over a decision. Should I hot-foot it up to Edgbaston to drink in an historic day or stay here and nurse my head? I considered shuffling around some lifts to put off my other duties but, in the end, the train timetable rendered it almost impossible and those extra couple of beers were too much for me to drive in the morning. In retrospect, I should have taken up the challenge of the Great British transport system. But the bigger mistake was deciding to agree to 'just one more' on a couple of occasions the night before.

Warwickshire were 25/4 in the first 12 overs with former England batsmen Jonathan Trott and Ian Bell becoming part of Sam Cook's eventual 3-42. Porter and Harmer shared the rest. Reportedly there was no champagne for the team after the game at Warwickshire but bubbly was sprayed for the cameras and waiting fans when the team arrived back at Chelmsford.

They would play the first couple of days of the penultimate game at Hampshire seemingly with a hangover. The home side compiled a regulation 254 in their first innings but, in reply, the champions-elect collapsed to 26/5 just before the end of day one. Kyle Abbott and Fidel Edwards did the damage, the former would add two more wickets inside four deliveries early on day two as Essex were bundled over for 76 and forced to follow on. It had been a sobering first six sessions. However, Lawrence and Bopara led a revival and, after a rain-affected third day, Foster and Wagner's 82-run partnership for the ninth wicket helped the visitors set Hampshire 185 to win, an incredible turnaround in itself. Then Essex found another entrant in their revolving door of match-winners. In only his third Championship game, Sam Cook blasted through the top order as the home side fell to 12/4 and then 37/7. When the paceman had Edwards caught behind in the 30th over it completed the most remarkable victory in a season that was filled with such success. It was a display of stoic determination given the title was already secure and it preserved the team's prized unbeaten record. Cook himself ended with figures of 11.4-6-18-5 as Hampshire were all out for 76, their lowest score since 1984. It was the first time Essex had won following on since 1999. That had been against Hampshire at Bournemouth, 25 years ago, the last year Essex had won the title.

The final game of the season was a procession. Yorkshire claimed the bowling points they need to stay up on day one in the process of dismissing Essex for 227. After that they folded. They were rolled over for 111 on day two and, after the new champions set them a highly unlikely 451 to win, were all out for a mere 76 with Cook taking 5-20.

It was a pretty pitiful performance from the visitors but perhaps I was the only Essex fan who cared. I had to leave Chelmsford in the middle of the afternoon to collect my daughter from school. Ordinarily, I could have begged a favour but, today, she was making her debut for the school netball team. It was probably her first-ever competitive match in any sport and it had dominated her thoughts for weeks. So, having watched the team all season and marvelled at their fairy-tale exploits, my personal story had a plot twist in the final act. I missed the trophy lift, the lap of honour and all the champagne-sprayed photographs that would greet me in the next day's papers. When Essex had last won the Championship I was still in full-time education, albeit the oldest possible end. That title was one of many. Not an after-thought but another fine victory by a hugely successful side that dominated the era.

Looking back, the 2017 season now seems almost surreal. It was so unexpected after years flattering to deceive in Division Two. The team had been revitalised almost immediately when the triumvirate of ten Doeschate, coach Chris Silverwood and chairman of the cricket committee Ronnie Irani took charge. It is hard to recount the tale from April to September without lacing it with inevitability. It never seemed that way. In fact, it only seemed a possibility when the team was extending their lead in the second part of the campaign.

Sport has dominated my life, both personally and professionally but I consider the 2017 County Championship as not only my favourite but my most important moment, partly for its merits but just as much because I desperately needed a joyful distraction at the time. Aside from the exploits of my favourite cricket team, 2017 was the worst year of my life. Again, this needs immediate qualification. No one died, no one was destitute. Actually, I was having one of my best ever financial years. My life was better than most of the UK but I was emotionally all at sea. I had been bold and brave in my career, eschewing the safe and securing and instead I followed the modern mantra of 'going for it'. Rightly or wrongly, I felt that gamble had failed. Having been out of the country for a couple of years, I had returned to the UK with fresh eyes. I saw an angry nation that did not know its own mind and was consistently undermined by the self-interest of the institutions that should be making it excel.

Depressed and feeling directionless, I did what a lot of middle-aged men do in such circumstances. I reverted to the comfort of what I knew. Initially, there was a reason for it. Those looking for reinvention in midlife are often urged to think back to what motivated them as a child. The wonderful *7-Up* documentaries produced by ITV, which have followed the lives of a group of children at seven-year intervals until they are pensioners, demonstrate this admirably. So often the broad pathways we use to plot our lives are set well before we reach our teenage years. Sport has always loomed large in my life, so much so I set out to make it my career. In a time of emotional turmoil it seemed natural to centre on it again. But football seemed too angry and greedy now while the England cricket team possessed an untouchable corporate sheen. County cricket still had a sense of decency, decorum and almost chivalry. It had its fair share of rude reprobates too but it had retained some qualities some other sports had lost in their upward trajectories. I had never truly left the county game but now I needed to nuzzle in its bosom once more.

And this most wonderful waste of time delivered. It offered up a season of unadulterated joy for my team and I. Chelmsford drew me further and further in as the season went on. The flexibility of my consultancy allowed me to see more games than any working man should. I sat there, forever alone but nearly always content. When I was not at the ground, my days were based around the online coverage. In the end, I tried to concertina my work before 11am or after 6pm on matchdays as I knew the distraction would be too much and I manoeuvred one major job so I would be able to watch the culmination of the campaign against Yorkshire.

This may sound strange and it could seem a vast over-reaction but I was swept along by the ever-growing story of success with a new cast of different characters. The distraction allowed me to adjust a little better to my new circumstances. My fear was that I had been fooling myself for decades and what I was experiencing now was cold, hard reality. Any previous success had been merely good fortune. In short, I had been found out. As the campaign wore on my mental chatter did not go away and, just as Essex started to seem assured of the title in August, I went to my doctor for some assistance. He recommended cognitive behavioural therapy (CBT) which would be administered by phone. The first call was a long list of introductory questions that I took in the Essex members' car park in Meteor Way. They had rung me while I was driving to a game and an interminable tally of queries was thrown at me by a therapist with an icy demeanour.

The call ran over, I missed the start of that day's play and ironically little made me more depressed than that in 2017. CBT was entirely ineffectual anyway. It involved talking, and I did not want to do that. I tried a few other wackier solutions, they were pointless too. I had done years of meditation. It was useful in taking the edge off the monotonous, self-defeating chatter in my head but my motivation was lacking. I exercised when possible but I had piled on weight while sinking lower and lower in the previous few years. The scales had always been a struggle and, if I am honest, a consistent precursor for a downward spiral. Yet, above everything, work was the key. Not money and not any old work either. As marketer and author Seth Godin calls it: 'Meaningful work for people who care.'

Although I was earning enough money consulting, I knew the security of a new career would suit me better. This meant applying for jobs, which led to constant rejection, more insecurity, plus networking, which I detested. It was that which cost me a trip to Edgbaston to see Essex finally haul themselves over the line and secure the title. That rankles. But missing the finale against Yorkshire and those effusive, first-in-a-generation celebrations has never truly bothered me.

My daughter's team got royally thumped in their netball tournament that afternoon, losing all three games by some margin against much older and more organised teams. They were in danger of being whitewashed until, it the last game, they finally squeezed in a glorious goal.

The joy on her face amid the jumping, smiling mass of pre-teen girlhood is my favourite sporting moment of 2017. Although, to be fair, that gloriously unexpected Championship victory by Essex CCC is a close second.

Cambridge MCCU v Essex
(and the unbeaten two)

Fenner's, 26 March 2019

A COUNTY'S first-class season normally begins with a friendly match against a university side. It is nearly always chilly and spectators are sparse. Critics would say this represents the perfect curtain-raiser for the County Championship season ahead.

The label of 'first-class' only exists for the purpose of the statistics, as this is a warm-up in every sense. The batting or bowling orders can be switched to accommodate the needs of the team and gerrymandered declarations often crowbar some competitiveness in on the last day.

I had never been to Fenner's and was unsure as to what to expect. In the end, it was a cosy venue, half of which was circled by functional, red-brick halls of residence for the university students. Behind a modest yet evocative wooden pavilion were buildings more in keeping your expectations of this famous seat of learning. The scene was an odd mix of gleaming spires, oak beams and squared-off student accommodation.

'So that's £5 for you and £5 for the car,' said the man on the gate as I pulled up. 'You can park by the boundary.'

That tenner gave me the rarest of opportunities, the ability to watch paid-for sport from my car. As I write these words I am sitting in my front seat with the back of my laptop leaning against the steering wheel at lunch on the first day with Essex 136/3. The scorecard presented to me at the gate denoted 'Sir' Alastair Cook as opening the batting. It was the first time I had seen a cricketing knight take to the field. He responded with a typically diligent, chanceless 50 in the morning session and would finish 150 not out as Essex hit 387/5 declared in their first innings of this three-day game. Cambridge replied with 176 then Nick Browne (98) and Ravi Bopara (55) led the visitors to 232/3 declared. Cambridge were bowled out for 157 to lose by 286 runs. Essex made sure all their frontline batsmen got time at the crease and their bowlers got in half-a-dozen overs. It felt like a friendly run-out with kit bags strewn across the boundary while players wandered in and out of the pavilion among the spectators.

University cricket was always a route into the first-class game. In the past, when higher education was more exclusive and elitist, it was a motorway rather than the B road it is today. This was the time of 'Gentlemen and Players' when amateurs had different gates on to the field and denotation on the scorecard. There were all sorts of tales and traditions maintaining social difference in the sport at the time. Thankfully most of them have disappeared but university cricket retains an elevated stature, especially at Oxford and Cambridge. The varsity clash is still played at Lord's and looking out on to the facilities at Fenner's it was hard not to be envious. I spent an age in the pavilion poring over the board listing university teams going back almost 100 years. Evocative names in gold letters stood out on the black backboards at the rear of the building. There was T.E. Bailey and D.J. Insole in 1947 and 1948, later of Essex and England. E.R. Dexter (1956), P.B.H. May (1952) and J.M. Brearley (1961) would all captain their country while H.C. Blofeld (1959) would look on from the commentary box. D.R. Pringle (1982) actually turned up a little later to watch his former sides from the boundary.

Cricket inside the mucky magnolia walls of my Essex comprehensive school in the 1980s seemed so far removed from the pristine pitches at Fenner's and nothing like tales of the public school game that pervade literature. The advantages afforded to the privately educated in cricket, in sport and in life are something of which I became increasingly aware as I got older. This is not about the individuals themselves, but the leg up in life that pupils receive. The material assets are the most obvious but, in my experience, the psychological advantages carry much more weight. I was a decent batsman with solid technique, a strategic sporting mind and patience. However, I lacked the temperament to bring the most out of those qualities. Insecurity allied to a propensity to overreact to errors and slights was fatal to my cricket and contributed greatly to fulfilling only a fraction of the minimal potential I possessed. The public schoolboys I faced on the pitch never seemed to have this problem. Similarly, when I interviewed candidates for jobs 20 years later, those whose grace under fire stood out were normally privately educated. They would charm their way through a poor answer or two and not be derailed. Even if they did not get the job, I would feel warmly disposed to them. It was a life skill I did not possess. Don't mistake this for a 'I could have been a contender' speech; my talent and psyche were far from sufficient for a career as a professional athlete. But I would have played at a much better standard had I gone to public school and almost certainly had a better career. It has been the lifelong ambition to write this book but I have prevaricated and procrastinated. Despite having written all my life and trained as a journalist, it is something that people like me just 'do not do', especially on such a personal topic. With three-quarters written and a firm offer on the table, I dithered for weeks over signing the contract, wondering whether I was merely embarrassing myself. It is no surprise that 'education, education, education' has become a political priority in Britain and the need for a better environment has led parents into all manner of moral minefields.

As my career ascended I met more and more former public school pupils in the upper echelons and found many apologetically aware of their background and certainly quick to point out if their entry was down to a scholarship rather than a cheque book. This is a horribly thorny issue and everyone's views are open to change. A few years ago, I read a book that set out to criticise the inequity of the public school system but, in the end, merely acted to confirm to me that it would have been worth taking out a second mortgage to fund my children's enrolment.

Having meandered aimlessly through much of my education, I fixed my sights on university only in the final year of my A-levels. The day I got into Newcastle is a 'JFK moment'. I was the first in my family to get to higher education, so I remember where I was and whom

I was with. Naïve, underconfident and uncool as it was feasible to be, I never went near the university cricket team on Tyneside. It was a wise decision as I was utterly outclassed by the aspiring Lancashire League players I encountered in intramural competition. My wicketkeeping was sufficient to get a grunt of approval but, batting-wise, I knew my place. In my first year, I shared a 74-run stand with a beanpole all-rounder from Blackburn. I contributed two, both singles from forward-defensive prods. These days you would probably describe it as 'Leachian'. Back then I felt not only that I played second fiddle but my partner was conducting an entire symphony on his own.

My sports-related Master's degree at Leicester University was different. I was a little older, a little more self-assured and mixed with some of what American students would call 'jocks'. I played casual cricket but declined a half-hearted invitation to try out for the second team as they were run by an exclusive public school clique and one member loudly declared, 'Well, that's the first psychological blow' when he broke our opening batsman's nose in an intramural game in which we were playing. I could do without the nastiness.

Now, in my middle age, I look back on this with great regret. My professor at Leicester had an esteemed reputation in his field. He was born to be academic given he was clever, always wished to argue and harboured for himself a healthy regard. He published books, spoke at conferences and went all around the world with his wisdom. Some would argue he never did a day's work in his life – he would reply that he pushed back the boundaries in his field. Yet he seemed as proud of his handful of games at a decent standard of non-league football as a lifetime of incisive sociological thought. We all want to 'do', not talk about, teach about or write about doing.

That's why those students in the light blue hats at Fenner's today should think themselves lucky. Whatever they do in their sporting careers from today, they can say they played against England's highest-ever run-scorer in a first-class game. They would be the last Cambridge students to have this honour as the label would be dropped later in the year. But, even if they just spent the three days chasing the ball to all parts and never played serious cricket again, it would still allow them to bask in a glimpse of the glory that Sir Alastair Cook has enjoyed.

Plenty of people sprinkle such information uninvited into conversations, those little asides that serve to reinforce their ego and impress their importance on the listener. I had noticed that I had started to do this in a working context. It was something I never used to do when I felt my career was on track.

Hampshire v Essex
(and the friend indeed)

Ageas Bowl, 5 April 2019

IT WAS cold, bloody cold and grey, battleship grey. The trip to Hampshire on the opening day of the season would require four warm, thick layers. Thinking about it, my top half attire was pretty much the same as I wore when skiing high up in the Colorado mountains a few years earlier. Having dropped the kids at school I hurtled round the M25 and down the M3. Inevitably, as I turned on to the M27 and closed in on the ground, the first dots of rain appeared on my windscreen.

Over the years, Hampshire's ground has become one of the county venues I most admire. This is partly because it is the model for a medium-sized county to become a major one, albeit with significant financial assistance, but mostly because I saw it develop from the ground up.

My first job in journalism was at the *Aldershot News* on the Hampshire and Surrey border. The sports team numbered three, including a bombastic sports editor with a drink problem. On my first afternoon, he poured something he had been storing behind his monitor into my coffee and whispered in my ear 'come on, let's make them Irish'. It was one of the very few times I have driven home in danger of being over the alcohol limit.

Still, I would learn a lot from this troubled, often difficult soul. He was a 'wind-up merchant' of a journalist, deliberately printing the most argumentative, pompous angle in banner headlines then 'fronting out' his stance using his natural eloquence. This ploy is still played out day after day, year after year on radio, television and in newspapers. It never seems to get old. This sports editor was talented in many areas but a master of this dark art. Decades later, I went to his funeral. The coffin was brought in by his former comrades from the parachute regiment. It was a nod to the young man he had been long before he became the irascible old fellow whose mistakes I sometimes mopped up. It was another lesson not to underestimate the older shells that remain when a person's youth has long departed. Those pall-bearers remembered a well-drilled soldier who jumped out of planes; I had only experienced a rather lazy yet still talented editor. As we filed out of the church, the sombre organ music that had supported the ceremony was suddenly punctuated by the hacksaw voice of Noddy Holder shouting 'Baby, Baby, Baaaaaaaaa-beeeeeee' and then the kerrang of chords as Slade's 'Cum on Feel the Noize' pumped out of the PA system. That summed up the man more than any eulogy.

I revelled in the cricket coverage at the paper, both professional and local, producing big spreads after the pre-season press days at The Oval and Northlands Road, Hampshire's old ground on the edge of Southampton. The two counties felt very different at the time. Surrey were the big London team, with a large ground, international stars and a huge history. Year after year, I scooped up a host of interviews and filled a few pages. It was one of the highlights of my journalistic year. I remember Alec Stewart being charming, polite and utterly professional, Adam Hollioake being charismatic and his late brother Ben sweet.

The Hampshire set-up was more parochial, less glamorous but my paper always seemed to have a closer relationship. They were slightly nearer, valued our attention a little more and I ghosted a column with Shaun Udal, a local product who was being touted as a future England off-spinner. These were the bad old days of too much chop-and-change in the minds of the selection committee. Udal would be picked in 1994 for a one-day international, which, back then, was often seen almost as a precursor of a Test call. His first five-day cap would arrive some 11 years later when he toured Pakistan and India. In the end, he would feature in four Tests, 11 ODIs and dismissed Sachin Tendulkar in his home country. He spent a couple of seasons at Middlesex as the sun set on his county career but he remains a Hampshire boy and, on the opening day of the 2019 season, I would look in at the suite that is named after him at the Ageas Bowl. A month or so later, it would emerge that Udal, who was born five months before me, had been diagnosed with Parkinson's disease; a fact that should put this book into perspective. Everyone feels they are fighting their own battle but, in truth, some are much more real and important than others. Best of luck, Shaun.

The abiding memory of all those Hampshire press days was chasing after Winston Benjamin for a 'quick word' as he strode across the Northlands Road pitch in the direction of the pavilion after the team group picture had been taken. The towering West Indian fast bowler immediately turned on his heels, folded his arms in defiance and gave me a look I have never quite forgotten. He said nothing for a few seconds and just glared. It was 80 per cent pretence and 20 per cent annoyance but I felt I just might be swatted over the boundary for six. I stammered out my request again and he gave me a decent five minutes. Then I scurried away grateful for never having to face his bowling. A few pre-seasons later, we were bussed out to a piece of hilly moorland at West End, a few miles outside Southampton. This was to be the site of the 'Rose Bowl', an ambitious new stadium and business development that would allow the club to host international games. I am writing this in the Colin Ingleby-Mackenzie Stand with Hampshire 215/3 at tea on day one of the 2019 season. Back on that heath in 1995 or maybe 1996, I interviewed Robin Smith, the powerfully built England No 3 batsman, and Udal on what we were told was going to become the square.

I made this trip to the south coast because I wanted to be present for the first ball of this County Championship season. As I have previously outlined, it seemed like the last chance to see this dear old competition in its natural habitat. Of course, obituaries have been written about the four-day game for more than half a century. Even at lunch today I would read a column by former Essex and England all-rounder Derek Pringle suggesting that the Championship was 'always under the cosh'. Coincidentally, I had passed the former cricketer-turned-journalist as I walked from my car to the ground this morning. He appeared to be carrying a box of his new book *Pushing the Boundaries*, which recounted his playing career through the 1980s. It was not lost on me as I hauled around a rucksack containing my laptop that this decorated international all-rounder and former national newspaper cricket correspondent was not averse to a little salesmanship to shift his book. I was intending to start writing in the stands once the match began but if anyone was going to read the finished work I would need to start hustling. At this stage, I still harboured doubts I could even get it off the ground.

Pringle fitted nicely into Essex CCC's squad of colourful characters 30 years ago. His path was typical – Felsted School and Cambridge University – but, after that, his career trajectory took an unusual turn. He balanced his studies with playing for Essex for four years and actually made his first-class debut against his own educational establishment. He was selected for England against India in 1982 while still an undergraduate. The publicity surrounding that and the inevitable but unfair comparisons with Ian Botham put him in the spotlight early on. He became a cult figure among Essex fans due to his unconventional taste in music, clothes and, heaven forbid, an earring. It was suggested that England selector Alec Bedser once told him to take it out as it would unbalance him at the crease. At times, it feels like more has been written about Pringle's earlobes than the bounce and swing he used to impart on the ball. Opposition fans often seemed to target him, perhaps because they expected more from a barrel-chested all-rounder measuring 6ft 4in. He seemed to tiptoe through his run-up and the bat looked like a matchstick in his hands. Certainly,

Pringle's international statistics belie the ability we saw at Essex for many years and may not have been helped by an inconsistent approach to selection in those days. However, having been at Headingley in June 1991 for arguably his most significant innings for England, he will always be one of my favourite characters on the county circuit. Pringle's piece this morning was right, it had felt like the 'Last Summer' for the Championship on numerous occasions. In fact, this book might have been a more straightforward tour of the Essex campaign had I not read Duncan Hamilton's book of that very title a few years earlier. Wonderfully written and very personal, he recorded the 2009 season at every level because he believed county cricket felt directionless. Clearly that was not true now but, in my opinion, we were hurtling the wrong way and the mapmakers seemed to have placed magnets on the compass.

The start of the county cricket season seemed to have much more significance when I was growing up. Aged ten or thereabouts, I remember putting the Essex team group on my wall after carefully unhooking it from the staples in the middle of *Tiger and Scorcher*. Every summer, the comic would publish pictures of all the county cricket squads. This always consisted of three rows of men in whites seemingly captured on a chilly day in late March. They were well presented by 1980s standards and you got to know their pasty faces, dubious sideburns and straggly hair. This was backed up by the obligatory *Playfair Cricket Annual*, daily coverage from the newspaper reports and those all-important scorecards. Deciphering these numbers was heaven for a sports-fixated teenage boy. The BBC's coverage of the John Player Sunday

League and one-day cups in midweek would then bring all these characters to life. On top of all that, there was the pinnacle – Test matches shown free-to-air throughout the summer. These days, some marketer would probably claim this to be a 'highly structured, tri-media approach targeting and engaging key demographics utilising the most authoritative messaging channels to develop the highest brand value'. I just thought I was reading about and watching sport I liked. There is much more media today and much more county content if you can be bothered to look for it. But it is not placed directly in the line of sight as it was back then. County cricket feels ignored these days. And, let's be honest, I should have had much better things to do today than drive a few hundred miles around Britain's motorway system for the privilege of sitting in the cold and watching cricket. I probably should have been developing my consultancy. The first couple of years have been profitable but demanding. A business like that needs constant hustle, all of it self-motivated. It was an endless exercise of plate-spinning where you obtain clients by creating content, speaking at events, advertising and constant coffee-fuelled networking.

This had never been the plan. Inspired by the back page of my father's *Daily Express*, my first and only real career-plan was to be a sports journalist. I started on that path and then veered off. Now even that diversion had been derailed. I read that when modern life gets meaningless you should revert to a previous one. The advice was to reconsider your pre-teen self, the person you were and what made you happy between the ages of eight and 12. For me, that was sport, mainly football and cricket. I had had enough of the former for now. The professional game in England had lost much of its morality and integrity. It used to be 22 men chasing a ball around a field for 90 minutes. Now it felt like 22 brands, representing two corporations chasing pound notes. That attitude had permeated the lower leagues and, most sadly of all, the youth football that my son was playing. The attitude of the game stank and, while I had lost many things, my sense of smell remained. At least cricket attempted to retain some sort of ethical code.

The embrace of the county game was familiar. I knew its history, its traditions, its charm, its courtesies and its meaning. I could turn up, sit there in the cold, talk to no one and everyone else would be OK with that. Perhaps that familiar anonymity was the reason I was at the Ageas Bowl this morning. Old men in overcoats were dotted over stands as if in a game of battleships, close to each other, but not right alongside. It was as if they wanted to sit in a communal group but did not actually want to communicate. I understood entirely.

I had arrived with a warm glow of optimism about 30 minutes before play was scheduled to start. There was a gentle hubbub in the spacious, airy pavilion as supporters became reacquainted after the winter, plus a dash of discernible excitement for the start of a new campaign. The main building at the Ageas Bowl is tall and topped with a tented roof reminiscent of the Mound Stand at Lord's. The views from the top tier offer not only a wonderful view of the game but also the rolling Hampshire countryside beyond. This had been an ambitious project and its journey had not always been smooth. There were financial issues and it became something of a local political football. Essex should have been the first visiting side but the Benson

& Hedges Cup tie in 2001 was rained off without a ball being bowled. Still, as I watched the opening overs of this 'last season' before The Hundred, it felt significant to be sitting in an arena that had allowed a county cricket club to change their story. Whether you liked what was planned or not, it was clear the domestic game in England needed to plot a new path and regain its former place in the sporting calendar.

But, at 11.21am under grey skies aided by the floodlights and in front of a few hundred spectators huddling against the cold, Essex began their season. Jamie Porter bowled the ball outside the off stump, Joe Weatherley left it. There had been a frustrating delay for bad light but, finally, we were under way. The mercurial medium pace of Ravi Bopara snagged James Vince lbw on the stroke of lunch to leave Hampshire 71/2. The talented Hampshire middle-order batsman was opening as it offered him the best chance of getting a place in the England side for the upcoming Ashes series. County finances are held up by revenue from the Tests but would another high-end sport see clubs adapt in such fundamental ways in the opening game of the season for the national good?

The lunchtime score flattered Essex but the afternoon session was truly brutal. Adding injury to insult, they even lost keeper Adam Wheater so Dan Lawrence filled in behind the stumps, pouching Aiden Markram off Matt Quinn's bowling. The Essex bowlers toiled away on a benign pitch only for Rilee Rossouw and then Sam Northeast to hoist them to all corners. The former's demise, caught on the deep midwicket boundary by a tumbling Simon Harmer, was an entirely self-inflicted dismissal as the pitch offered little.

As I have said, the Ageas Bowl is among my favourite grounds on the county circuit. But the reasons are more than just sentiment. Access is so easy. You can drive in, park outside and walk less than a hundred yards to the entrance turnstile. For county games, a concourse allows you to promenade the circumference of the arena with relatively few obstructions of the field. The site had been developed even further since I was last there and a hotel had popped up opposite the main stand and bowlers were now described as delivering from the Hilton End. The design allowed cricket patrons to access the same bar and catering facilities as hotel guests but from a different side. I watched much of the afternoon session nursing a coffee and peering through the window as Northeast and Rossouw broke loose.

Word had gone around that Liverpool FC were staying over ahead of their visit to Southampton that night. Members of the BBC commentary team even mentioned seeing some of the stars wandering around the hotel before play had commenced. It is curious to wonder what the likes of midfielder Sadio Mane, of Senegal, and Egyptian striker Mo Salah would have thought of county cricket had they poked their heads through their curtains on this rather turgid afternoon. These were among the most famous people in their countries and would make a similar shortlist for the entire African continent. For them, sport was fast, rich and raucous, played out in front of full stadia and in the glare of public interest. Even for a lifelong devotee such as myself, the start of the 2019 County Championship campaign was low-key and somewhat tedious. Cold and slightly dispirited, I left midway through the final session. Bad light ended play shortly afterwards.

On day two, Hampshire eventually declared on 525/8 with Northeast contributing 169. Then they dismissed Essex for 164. Sir Alastair Cook top-scored with 50, the first ever Championship innings by a serving knight. Essex fared little better following on. They were all out for 274 to lose by an innings and 87 runs. Bopara trumpeted his personal form with a 107 and Harmer would contribute 62. In total, six different wicketkeepers were used in this game with both sides' regular glovemen picking up injuries and an outfielder filling in until a replacement be called in. Hampshire's Lewis McManus was halfway through a round of golf when he got told to grab his kit and get to the ground. He would pick up four catches in the second innings. South African Kyle Abbott took 5-77 as the visitors' resistance crumbled on the final day. A few months later his ability to extract life from the pitch at the Ageas Bowl would make a timely contribution to the Essex push for the title. But, for now, it had been a chastening opening to the season.

The Friend Indeed

Friendship is often a difficult topic for a middle-aged man to discuss.

The concept of deliberately and openly cultivating non-sexual companionship jars with many. Perhaps it harks back to early playground insecurity when the constant possibility of rejection created a troubling vulnerability. The TV comedy *The Inbetweeners* brilliantly skewered the issue with its main characters, a group of crude, awkward teenagers, constantly ridiculing each other for going to extra effort to make new acquaintances. 'Oooohh, fwiends!' they would coo to each other in a condescending voice when one of the group spoke about an outsider. Belittling derision is often the way young men exert control over each other.

For many of us, this sort of uncomfortable, deep-seated emotion bubbles up once more when we think about friendship in middle age. Therefore we avoid it. Often the very notion has been squeezed out in order to accommodate the demands of family and work. The excuses are easy: it is just too much effort, I'm too tired and I have too many responsibilities. Certainly, this was the case with me. As soon as I bought my first property the ardour of alcohol-based night-time adventures lost much of their allure. Others had already retreated after coupling up and the pace of withdrawal only increased when children came along. I would follow suit soon after. An all-embracing, life-consuming job sucked up any remaining energy. However, in my case, a constant desire to change and advance also led to me cutting off close friends in a way I thoroughly regret. But the same old conversations, based around high-jinks at school, parroting TV comedies and re-runs of well-worn topics was just not enough anymore.

Still, just like the message on mental health, the acute and detrimental effects of loneliness is now a topic of open discussion. In 2015, the Office of National Statistics suggested these feelings afflicted one in seven people between the ages of 45 and 54. US researchers likened the harmful effects of loneliness to smoking 15 cigarettes a day. It sounded like a tabloid twisting serious science but, apparently, it was broadly valid. They defined loneliness as the inability to discuss 'intimate and highly personal feelings with someone', which means, as we all know, you can be popular, have a rich social life, a big family, be married and still be lonely.

In 2015, a *Guardian* report summed it up this way: 'Middle age is that phase of life in which our possibilities and freedoms seem to contract most dramatically, where our sense of who we are and will be is liable to feel most constrained by pressures from all sides. The disappointments and anxieties of unfulfilling work, unhappy family life, and our own or others' poor health are intensified by the conviction that there is no escape: this is simply the hand fate has dealt us. It's not hard to imagine what a lonely feeling that can be.'

From the time we leave education, we are making decisions that seem to peel away layers of our potential. Finally, you have to earn your own money so you have to decide on a path and then double down. After that one goes through the long list of choices Ewan McGregor's Renton trots out at the start of the film *Trainspotting*, from 'a family' to 'electrical tin openers' and everything in between.

It is doubtful that any of us has made every choice correctly and, gradually, the torture of comparison can creep into your mind. This is where the internet and especially social media has been a multiplier. Now, in your darkest moments, you can easily find updates from that kid who made school a nightmare or the person from work who lifted themselves up on the back of your efforts. And sometimes you feel a prick of anger or jealousy, then a measure of regret, if you perceive them to have been more successful than you.

A career crossroads such as mine allows space for such regrettable, unpleasant thoughts to persist. In part, county cricket helped fill this self-created void which, in turn, led to this book.

I would sit in contented solitude in the crowd at Chelmsford watching my team toil away. All around me were people – mostly men, mostly of pensionable age, mostly on their own. The flow of the game filled my thoughts and the BBC Essex commentary team were my conversation. A simple, satisfactory arrangement went on for years. I went to the place where Essex were playing, I paid, sat in the stands on my own, they played, I drank coffee, they stopped playing, I went home. My only conversation was to ask a server for the warm drink and say 'Thank you' for the change.

Then something quite odd occurred. A very close school friend, someone I had known for almost 40 years, declared an interest in cricket. This was an unexpected revelation. In PE, he possessed precisely one shot, a hoik to cow corner. This was one more than most of the boys at the hessian-covered Essex comprehensive school I endured, therefore he was far from the last player chosen through the traditional *Usual Suspects*-style line-up at the start of the class. He had married early and emigrated to a far-away cricketing country. We kept in touch as old friends do but time, distance and different paths created an emotional gap.

His life changed a few years ago and when he visited England once again, I sensed he was having his own middle-age reassessment and trying to plan a path forward for the rest of his life. This was entirely in keeping with the thoughtful, formative man I knew well during the first few decades of his life. What I did not expect was for him to ask me to go to see the fourth day of the fifth

Test against India at The Oval on 10 September, 2018. He wanted to see Alastair Cook's last innings for England. 'Chef' was 46 not out overnight and the country's greatest batsman had the chance of a fabulous farewell. He had started his career with a century against India, and 12 years later, the Essex left-hander could complete his journey with superb symmetry.

I must admit I dithered when my friend texted me the night before with the news that tickets were still available. Childcare duties meant that I would only be able to be there until lunch so Cook had to stay in and score at least 54 runs in the morning session. There was moisture in the pitch and he had ridden his luck the previous day. He could last one ball and it would all be over. But the nightmare scenario was having to leave at the interval with Sir Alastair knee-deep in the nervous 90s. I was not sure I could call on some cheeky favours from fellow parents in such circumstances.

We texted back and forth and then, just before bedtime, I decided to gamble. It would cost me £42 and a whole heap of hassle but the pay-off could be history. The memory that tipped me over the edge was from my father, who had been at The Oval for the fifth Test against Australia 70 years earlier when legendary Australian batsman Don Bradman required just four in his final game to retire with an average of 100. In one of sport's greatest ever letdowns, leg spinner Eric Hollies bowled 'The Don' for a second-ball duck. As a result, 99.94 has become an iconic sporting number.

'He came out to a standing ovation,' my father recounted many times. 'And, a few minutes later, walked back to … ab-so-lute … silence.'

Many other cricket fans had also spotted the same opportunity. It was a saga travelling to The Oval and a drama collecting the tickets we had purchased online. But that will end up on the cutting room floor of my movie when I tell the tale in years to come. We were sardined at the back of the OCS Stand. The ground was packed and the atmosphere hummed with the special excitement of thousands who had said 'sod it' to themselves the night before and cleared their Monday by fair means or foul. Cook's every run was over-cheered and a rare dangerous moment was 'ooooohhhhh-ed' to within an inch of its life. I had only a cursory interest in the game as a whole; England had won the series anyway. My concern was solely Cook's score and the clock. It would be close but he always seemed set to meet my personal deadline. Fifteen minutes from lunch, Cook nudged a single off Ravindra Jadeja to go to 97 but Jasprit Bumrah's aberrant, unnecessary throw added an extra four to his score. The error meant it was not quite the Hollywood moment anyone had hoped for. However, this was a batsman whose talent was always measured in reliability, responsibility and sheer weight of runs rather than individual moments of inspiration. There are players whose exploits make for a better highlights reel on YouTube but we all know who we would prefer to open the batting. Cook's England career can be reflected upon with long-term admiration, rather than short-term awe. We stood, we cheered, we shared the moment. It might not be quite so iconic as my dad's Bradman tale but I'll bore someone about it someday I'm sure.

His innings would end on 147 and his Test career on a grand total of 12,472 runs. He had long since passed the second name on the list, another Essex legend, Graham

Gooch, with 8,900. Incidentally, third place goes to Alec Stewart with 8,463, which incredibly also represents the day of his birth – 8 April 1963. It is perhaps my favourite sporting statistic.

About the time Cook edged Hanuma Vihari to Rishabh Pant and left the crease for the last time as an England player, I was waiting for my daughter to emerge from a small Hertfordshire primary school. Little did she know that between drop-off and pick-up, after her assembly and just before the lunchtime bell rang, I had created a memory that will be cherished forever. Better still, I shared it with my friend. After all these years, I had discovered a new side to him, one that I was happy to nurture.

A few weeks later, I took him to an Essex game. It was the first time I had been 'with' anyone to Chelmsford since my father had died over a decade earlier. County cricket had become a solo sanctuary for me, a place where I was content to be lonely in a crowd. It felt different yet pleasant. My friend was now on the upside of his own life-trough a couple of years earlier. I admired his capacity for reinvention, openness and positivity. It seemed strange for me to introduce the characteristics of the Essex players and explain some of the nuances of the county game to a very old acquaintance yet cricket-spectating newbie.

As ever, the soporific cadence of the match lent itself to candour and we chatted freely about deeper topics that troubled us. For a self-confessed communication 'clam', it felt liberating. It was also comforting to reconnect warmly with the past. One's oldest friendships always tend to last the longest. That may be because we are comfortable playing our old familiar roles. Playground self-perception can be impossibly hard to shake off. I have moved many times for work and university, often feeling it was better to leave friendships in, what I thought to be, their proper place and time. Perhaps that was self-justification for a plain old defence mechanism. This friend was from way back, from school, so despite stretching the sinews on our connection, often living on the other side of the world and sometimes going years without talking, we never lost touch. Selfishly, he was also the sensible, soulful sounding board I needed right now. Unfortunately, the season ended before we could squeeze in another game. But there was hope of more stolen afternoons together in the 2019 season. We connected casually over the winter and our next major conversation also coincided with cricket. Only the tone would be very different.

Wheater's injury at Hampshire caused a lengthy delay in play on the opening day of the county season. First he got treatment, then went off and Lawrence had to don pads and gloves. It all took time. However, this little drama entirely eluded me on the day. Just after Wheater called for assistance my phone rang so, as courtesy demands, I scuttled under the stands at the Ageas Bowl and away from the watching supporters to take it. It was my newly cricket-loving but old friend. There was news.

He recounted a tale that, unbeknownst to me, had unfolded over the winter. Suffice to say it was a sudden, serious and complicated story. It precipitated an immediate and unexpected change for him and had led to one of the most testing periods of his life. However, in the months that followed, his situation gradually improved and he began planning out a future for himself once more. Happily, he was clear about his path, one that would probably mean a return to that far-away land. I was pleased for him but retained a pang of selfish disappointment. Friendships are more fleeting as you get older; some people even compartmentalise 'work friends' and 'real friends' on the assumption that everyone will just move on when they change jobs. As mentioned, I am guilty of both this and the crime of pushing away potential confidants. I am an introvert who is mostly content with my own company. At least that is the story I tell myself.

But, for a summer and with cricket as an unlikely backdrop, I happily reconnected with a friend from a former life and talked more freely than I had in years. Our conversation made me realise how the rigours and expectations of modern life had left me in some form of self-isolation. In 2020, Brene Brown, the 'human connection' researcher whose TedTalk on 'The Power of Vulnerability' has been viewed almost 50 million times, discussed this topic on the Tim Ferriss podcast. She argued that, as we grow older, the 'armour' that has thus far protected us from trauma and disappointment no longer serves its purpose and starts to hold us back. The ability to adapt and change your mindset was, in her view, the 'most important developmental milestone of midlife' and the failure to do so was normally a 'slow, brutal unravelling' rather than a crisis. This rang true. Actually it rang loud, clanging alarm bells.

When this happens, the power of friendship was more important than ever, certainly more than in childhood, adolescence or early adulthood. Back then reinvention always seemed possible. There was the eternal option of locating to another friend, partner, job or town. But, in middle age, the extraction of long-established roots would be far too painful if it was even possible at all. The process of turning potential into reality had meant making decisions and, inevitably, closing off certain opportunities. For the most part, this is a positive process. Society preserves a particular sadness for the fifty-something who continually hangs on to a millennial sensibility. That is why we feel we have to make those *Trainspotting* choices, often when we are far too immature and open to external influences. In the past few decades, 'No Regrets' and 'No Fear' have become T-shirt slogans. Nike even turned 'Just Do It' into a rallying call to sell trainers. But people are fearful, they do have regrets and unthinking action can lead to long-term anguish.

It is then that you need an old friend with whom to talk. Someone who will listen, not just wait for their turn to speak. Someone who will help you sift through your mental chaff to find an ear of wheat. Someone with whom you have history: good and bad but always shared. Therefore someone whose thoughts you are prepared to accept. Connection is easy these days, advice is abundant, very little of it is worth your time. After he went back to that far-flung cricketing land, though I had barely been in the same room for a dozen days in the last decade, I missed my friend more than I ever had before.

Surrey v Essex
(and the blazing blue bats)
The Oval, Friday, 12 April 2019

AROUND 30 minutes after I arrived on day two, Alastair Cook, sorry Sir Alastair Cook (we were all still getting used to that), tickled the ball to the keeper and departed for an ignominious 11 to leave Essex 20/1. Nick Browne would follow him a few minutes later. The visitors were in serious trouble in the wake of Surrey's 395 all out when they sloped in for lunch shortly afterwards.

The skies were light grey in south London as I peered down at the worrying finale to the morning session. It was slightly better weather than the Ageas Bowl the previous week, but an overcoat was still required. This was Surrey's first game since lifting the title the previous September. They are perceived as the richest and best-supported county; the first day of this game was attended by a healthy 2,500 supporters. This did not feel like a desolate few sessions in the shires attended by one man, one woman, one flask and two cups. However, it was still a world away from my last visit to The Oval with my old friend, but new cricket buddy, when Cook made history. At that point, the Championship-winning pennant was flying from the top of the pavilion at Chelmsford after Ryan ten Doeschate's men had so gloriously and surprisingly lifted the title a year earlier. They had gone unbeaten throughout the 2017 season and Surrey were set to achieve the same feat until they met Essex in the final game of the campaign at The Oval.

I was not there for the game so I can't say whether it was a Surrey hangover after securing the title or just that Essex played darn well. But the visitors rolled them over for 67 and then ran up 477/8 declared. Surrey responded like champions with 541 in their second innings, leaving Essex chasing 134 to secure the sort of record-scuppering victory in which supporters delight. No team had ever conceded a 410-run first-innings lead and gone on to win but Surrey looked likely to achieve history when No 11 Matt Quinn joined ten Doeschate at the crease at 124/9. However, Essex squeezed home in another remarkable story authored by their redoubtable captain. At times it would be spikey with South African fast bowler Morne Morkel peppering Quinn, a real tailender, with short-pitched balls in the final stages.

As that season-ending nail-biter was unfolding the 18 county chairmen were meeting just yards away in The Oval's inner sanctum with The Hundred top of their agenda. Cricinfo reported that the atmosphere was fractious, particularly over the news that costs for the new tournament had trebled. The meeting overran, preventing ECB chairman Colin Graves from presenting the County Championship trophy to Surrey captain Rory Burns. It was ironic as the last five years of the competition had seen a host of different teams take the prize with the drama continuing often to the final day. The old, historic tournament seemed to have been getting better and better in the last decade. Yet, increasingly, one felt this did not seem to matter.

All that was far from my mind today. I doubt that many matchday experiences will be better than that of Surrey this season. If Hampshire CCC is the most improved county set-up in the last generation, moving from tidy, traditional ground to Test and World Cup host, then The Oval is the venue that has made the most of its long-standing advantages. This is a moneyed county, reaping huge benefits from its metropolitan location and Test match status. However, the club were still doing the little things right.

This game was in the first week of the Easter holidays so, among the city suits and M&S beige, there were a few kids and dads. At the intervals, everyone was not so much invited as implored by the PA announcer to get on the pitch. The youngsters could have cricket sessions with coaches and the club mascot in one area, you could watch the players net in another and the rest of us pretended to have an informed look at the pitch. The wifi worked well, the stewarding was friendly and efficient, even the concessions were reasonably priced. It remains a special place to watch cricket, firmly in my top three trips along with Trent Bridge and Lord's. There are an increasing number of 'have-nots' in English cricket. Essex were better than that, a 'have-some' perhaps. Surrey were certainly a 'have' but at least they were using some of their money to create a better matchday experience. One that could provide a 'big event' atmosphere on an occasion such as Cook's Test farewell but also provide intimacy and atmosphere for a less attended match like that of today.

At lunch, I examined the pavilion. The County Championship trophy was proudly displayed in a glass case just inside the entrance and backlit to stand out in the darkened corridor. My emotions were mixed about seeing it there. To my utterly partisan mind, they had 'taken it' from Essex and, as '$urrey' were the Manchester United of the county game, I would prefer to see it anywhere but there. However, the presentation suggested this gleaming gold pot had pride of place in their organisation. It was truly cherished. From there, the staircase twists around towards two top tiers but there are bars or restaurants overlooking the pitch on many floors en route. Other doors lead to offices. The Oval is a historic venue and when I first walked through the gates midway through the morning session, several guided tours were starting up. On this particular day, the line was longer for the fish and chip stall a few yards away but, still, you were clearly in a special place.

Essex would recover from their precarious lunchtime position thanks to a crucial 96-run stand between Dan Lawrence and Tom Westley. After a humbling defeat at Hampshire in their opening fixture and an equally dispiriting first day of this game which ended with Surrey 342/7, the keyboard warriors of social media were out in force overnight. Lawrence had announced himself with 161 at The Oval as a 17-year-old four summers ago to become the third-youngest Championship centurion. In the afternoon, he played watchfully, especially off his legs, and exploited the short boundary on one side of the wicket with a series of punchy fours. He would fall seven runs short of a century but he had done his job. Rishi Patel, on debut as replacement for the injured Ravi Bopara, played stylishly for 31 before being caught by Rikki Clarke off Tom Curran. On-loan keeper Rob White would also chip in with 39. Deep into the afternoon session, Lawrence was joined by ten Doeschate, who would take his Championship career average to 80 against Surrey with a typically combative 130 from 166 deliveries. The Dutchman, who had relinquished the Twenty20 captaincy to Simon Harmer over the winter, is a specialist in delivering quick, match-turning innings when it really matters. His century at The Oval, plus some late-order tenacity, took Essex to 448 all out, a lead of over 50 and provided the slightest sniff of victory.

However, the pitch was too docile and Surrey batted well to see off the danger. The game limped to a solid draw. These were the last two champions and they were evenly matched on this occasion. After an emphatic opening round defeat, Essex needed that sort of validation. These teams were favourites for the 2019 title and, on this showing, there was every possibility of a close battle. If any season needed an attention-grabbing race for the County Championship trophy then this was it.

The blazing blue bats

Essex v Middlesex, Royal London One-Day Cup, 19 April 2019

For the last few seasons, I have bought my children a membership of Essex CCC. It barely registers with them but, as a sporting father, I explain this to myself as a long-term investment. I hope that by osmosis, telepathy, boredom or sheer bloody-mindedness the game will seep into their skins. There is no point in inflicting a four-day game on them. Meanwhile, Twenty20 games are too packed, too beery, too sweary and there will be little change from £200 as these tickets are not part of a county membership. However, games in the original one-day format are included so we always go as a family to an early-season fixture.

The agenda for the day is straightforward. Knowing that my pride will not last a full game, we time our arrival to exploit the highlight of their day – the interval. Strange as it may seem, the break in play is when they engage the most with cricket. It is because they are allowed on the pitch to play the game themselves. I do not know another sport that permits spectators on the field during a break. On occasion, I have seen youngsters on the court after NBA basketball games in the USA and it is common to see organised exhibition games with youngsters during half-time in football matches. But this is open to everyone; all you need is a bat, a ball and some enthusiasm. As a kid, there is nothing like getting on the pitch during the game to replicate what you have been watching so far. Even if you do not understand what has been going on. You can keep all the expertly researched, wonderfully executed schemes by experienced marketers, this is the single factor that brings my children closer to the game. With dead eyes and arms folded, they will gloomily tolerate me explaining why those discs are important, why the umpires are engaging in some sort of semaphore and why the wicketkeeper is sometimes close to the stumps and sometimes far away.

But that all changes when the first innings is over. Suddenly a swarm of children clamber over the fence and start smashing orange balls to all corners with bright blue bats. Every important health and safety law is broken as mini-games smother the outfield and balls whistle around from all directions. The big kids are enthusiastic too. Grandparents accompany little ones and you can imagine they feel the effects of unleashing a long-retired bowling action for days to come.

At the midpoint of the Middlesex game, my two were among the first on the pitch and set their square to the right of the scoreboard. In the first round, my son batted, my daughter bowled, I kept wicket and my wife was at mid-off. Whisper it quietly, but I am actually a qualified cricket coach. It is only the first award and I got it around 25 years ago down in Eastbourne under the tutelage of Neil Lenham, who was playing for Sussex at the time and the son of coaching doyen Les. My class included Steve Gatting, a former Brighton footballer whose brother Mike had been England cricket captain a few years earlier. It was a hugely rewarding experience. We were there to learn how to pass the rudiments of the game on to colts. If they needed further tuition or we wanted to coach adults, we had to take a further course. Crucially, we were told to avoid coaching out natural ability. 'If he holds the ball like he is eating an apple but turns it square then let him be.' This was the opposite of the Football Association badge I passed at the same time, which was full of needless regimentation and schoolmasterly faux-discipline.

Even now, I can recall enough to teach the fundamentals of batting and bowling to a total novice. This I do on the pitch during a break in a one-day game at Chelmsford every single year. As neither of my children are yet in their teens, I reckon I have another two years of acting this way before they start to ignore me or deliberately execute the opposite of my instructions.

As a stickler for accuracy and achievement, my daughter will concentrate hard to implement her bowling action. She looks quite cute too and a couple of years earlier she was singled out by the community coaches who were wandering around with young bowler Aaron Beard as part of a club promotion. With photographers and cameramen in attendance she furrowed her brow, stuck out her tongue in concentration and bowled very competently. She is one of those little girls who wants to get everything right. My son listens too but, in the end, just tries to thwack the ball as hard and as far as he can. Despite my best efforts, his bowling action is eccentric. It is not exactly Paul Adams' frog-in-a-blender but may be derived from the same species. But that is the serious sporting father speaking. Today, I had had my 'Bank Holiday Barbecue' head on. We had fun. It was nice. That's enough. A clever cricketing father merely hopes to leave a positive memory. If you can build up a bank of those then you have a chance.

This was a particularly sunny Good Friday. The official crowd was just over 3,000, the biggest in four years at Chelmsford for the 50-over competition. Arriving late, we had little option but to settle for cooped-up bucket seats by the side of the main scoreboard. This was the non-members' part of the ground and traditionally noisy. The weather, the four-day weekend and, hopefully the cricket, brought out a group of lads intent on drinking their way through the afternoon. No problem there. My kids considered this part of the show. When we first arrived they were in deep discussion with one of the security staff. This was not an alcohol-related misdemeanor. It was because they had brought in a St George's Cross with Alastair Cook's name in one corner and draped it over a sponsor's sign. They had been asked to take it down. If the game was live on television and the company involved had the chance for much wider visibility it might have been understandable. But this seemed a little churlish. After some edgy but polite negotiations, the lads eventually relented. It would be straight back up after the interval when, incongruously enough, former Essex and England bowler John Lever would sit down in the middle of the group and watch for a while.

The lads had decamped on the pitch at the break for their own loud, hard-hitting game. Their ball was soft-ish but a forceful blow in the face would have left an adult sore and a child with a tearful shock that might have ended their afternoon. With balls bouncing all over the outfield, every parent has one eye on their own game and the other on everyone else. This can be troubling given that these impromptu matches possess batters with vastly differing abilities, pre-school children barely able to wield their willow to club players trying all manner of audacious shots to impress their mates. In the end, the games passed off safely. It is always a minor relief to have negotiated this hectic half-hour having given your children a positive experience and, secondly, not suffered or seen any injuries. The pre-interval announcements studiously spell out that spectators are entering the pitch 'at their own risk'. However, those ambulance-chasing injury lawyers on television tell us that 'where there's blame, there's a claim'. We have seen such blows in other sports lead to compensation payouts. Quite how a club can effectively police all this is beyond me, apart from those crystal clear announcements spelling out that 'ye enter here at your own peril'. One cannot help but think we are a major injury from this being banned. Such interval excursions were no longer possible at Twenty20 games after the first few years. Time was the key factor in this instance, fair enough given that the pace of play is at the centre of this version of the sport. Of course, the other factor is the potential for inebriated antics from a certain section of the crowd. It would be a recipe for disaster.

Middlesex rattled up an ominous 366/8 in their 50 overs thanks to 95 from Dawid Malan and 63 off 30 balls from George Scott towards the end. It was one run short of their highest 50-over total ever. A century from Varun Chopra, his second in successive games, and 77 from Tom Westley put Essex in the hunt midway through the reply. But their departures were part of a middle-order slump that cost the home side the game.

Nearly 700 runs were scored on the day. High-scoring, high-factor sunblock and high attendance would be replicated on the day up and down the country on Good Friday. There were 5,000 at Sussex, Yorkshire and Somerset along with the 3,000 at Chelmsford. These figures became ammunition to fire at the cricket authorities as, in the week before the start of the Royal London 50-over competition, Gordon Hollins, then ECB's new county cricket managing director, predicted the event would be 'a development competition' in 2020. It was already public knowledge that the longer short-form competition would be contested while the new event took centre stage. The irony was that after a lot of experimentation, 'the' one-day format was firmly established at 50 overs. Previously, the ECB had mandated the domestic competition follow suit to strengthen England's chances in international competition, especially the World Cup, and this summer the tournament was back on home soil for the first time since 1999. Tickets were very expensive and, as I discovered the previous week, very sold out. Only the cricketing outpost of Durham had any range of availability. Down south, my only option was Afghanistan v Bangladesh at the Ageas Bowl for £75. No, thanks. So, at this point in the campaign, it felt as if we were in the strange, unsatisfying situation of hosting the globe's most prestigious cricket competition using a format that would not be played at county level in England the following season.

The 50-over competition of 2020 was likely to be a mixture of second XI players and those first-teamers not required by The Hundred. This had knock-on effects. At present, the Royal London Cup was an important benefit of my membership so should I assume the price would be reduced given that the product has gone down in quality? Also, judging by the pints, chips and ice creams being consumed at Chelmsford on Good Friday, there was significant food and beverage income from 3,000 people watching a seven-hour game. Still, the teething troubles of an unnecessary tournament were not my primary thoughts as Essex started their reply against Middlesex on this gorgeous Good Friday. My daughter was the focus.

As a diligent, meticulous, intelligent child, she had taken a liking to scoring. I introduced it a couple of years before and the addition of different-coloured pens for individual bowlers sealed the deal. We scored 15 overs, just enough to start discussing trends from the statistics we had created. There are many routes into cricket and I was taking the 'whatever works' approach. I'd figured out that my son might be attracted by the brash, big-hitting IPL, so I'd been watching as much as possible on television. It was starting to scratch the surface. But he is a 12-year-old boy who prefers playing to watching any sport, even football.

After much negotiation we agreed to leave at the 30-over point of the Essex innings. As we got up, an elderly gentleman remarked on our early departure. 'Can't keep them in their seats,' I replied with a smile. As we walked back around the ground, other kids of a similar age were watching and it crossed my mind to forcibly 'stick it out' in the hope they start to engage with the sport. But those days are gone. It is better for these early touch points with the game to be positive. Unlike me, they already had a kaleidoscope of entertainment options at their fingertips. Growing up, my television had just four channels but now they could already make their own choices. Honey succeeds more often than vinegar but in a digital world it is the only option. It teaches your children to be nicer people too.

My son has talked of 'playing cricket because Dad did'. I have steered him away from that notion. However, as we left the ground at the Hayes Close End I did point out the place he has to drop me off at about 10.45am when I am deep in retirement and no longer walk so well. 'Just pick me up about 6-ish,' I added. As long as I have the right clothing, refreshments and entertainment devices I'll be fine. But the company of my son or daughter would be best of all.

This was the dutiful role I performed for my father in his later, more incapable years. After collecting him and driving to the ground, I would negotiate a swift turnaround with the steward at the New Writtle Street entrance so I could drive in, pull out his wheelchair and position him just to the right of the executive boxes. I would then drive off and park on Moulsham High Street before running back to join him for the day.

Then we watched. Sometimes speaking but mostly in silence. It did not really matter about the opponents, the importance of the game or the state of the perennial and usually ill-fated promotion push that Essex were in the midst of undertaking. It was all a wonderful waste of time but I am glad we spent that time together. To this day, every time I walk past the entrance at the Hayes Close End, I think of my father.

Post script: When we returned home after the game, my son called me out in the garden to play cricket. He wanted to practise his batting. He said his motivation was PE at school. They would be playing cricket this summer and he did not want to be embarrassed. Whatever the reason, I am taking this as a little victory. My son asked me to play cricket with him. That will do for now.

* * *

The defeat to Middlesex would be the first of six in the Royal London Cup. Chopra had starred with a century in the opener as Essex crushed Glamorgan by 180 runs. Then, following that run-fest on Good Friday, ten Doeschate's men would lose to Surrey and Somerset. The skipper shared a partnership of 150 with Ravi Bopara against Hampshire at Chelmsford as both batsmen finished on 89 in a sizeable total of 341. The visitors could only muster

230. However, defeat to Sussex off the penultimate ball stymied the possibility of making the knockout phase. They lost games against Kent and Gloucestershire to finish second-bottom in the South Group. It had been a disappointing 50-over campaign. At the end of it, a report in *The Cricketer* magazine added: 'Set in the foreground of Essex's poor start to the season is the feeling of discontent around the club. There are rumours of a fractured dressing room, accentuated by captain Ryan ten Doeschate being dropped for the final two games of the One-Day Cup. Fans meanwhile are growing increasingly irate at the poor displays and lack of fight.'

Supporters would be similarly vocal for the first half of the team's Vitality Blast campaign when results were also pitiful. They would turn that around in spectacular style. Having no knowledge of the dressing room dynamic apart from what was in the press, I can have no informed opinion here. But it has always been clear that, like any achievement, sporting success is never a smooth ascent. End-of-season accounts such as this cannot help falling into the inevitable groove where the 'great men of history' theory resides. My favourite Essex CCC book, *Summer of Success*, told its tale in this fashion. Inevitably, this book will do the same to a certain extent. Every victory is recounted as A led to B led to C, when often they went via J then Q with a major row at V, a dressing down back at F before a host of injuries and personal problems at M.

The Royal London One-Day Cup Final would be played between Somerset and Hampshire on 25 May. It was billed as the 'Last Lord's final' as Trent Bridge would host the denouement of the degraded competition in 2020. There was to be no send-off either. A World Cup warm-up game between England and Australia was scheduled for the same day. I spent most of that Saturday flicking between the two games on television.

There was a clear counterpoint between the two fixtures. The Royal London Cup Final was won by Somerset. It was hardly a classic nor even much of a contest. Hampshire's 244/8 from their 50 overs would have won many Benson & Hedges Cup Finals, the 55-over tournament that was abolished in 2002, or Friends Provident Cup Finals, the 60-over event that was the traditional showpiece of the season until 2009. However, the one-day discipline had advanced so much since then, especially after the introduction of the Twenty20. Somerset simply put together a composed chase and won with ease.

This year's tournament had seen a raft of 300+ scores and one 800+ game between Nottinghamshire and Lancashire. It all seemed so long ago that I stood on the streets outside Lord's for the famously free-scoring 1994 NatWest Final between Sussex and Warwickshire. I was flogging *JM96** (aka *Johnny Miller 96 not out*), one of the first established cricket fanzines. After answering an ad in *When Saturday Comes*, its slightly more serious football equivalent, I had been writing for them regularly and got to know the editor reasonably well. My brief was covering two counties, Essex of course, and Leicestershire, where I was studying at the time.

By 1993, I was at the University of Brighton, starting my studies for a PhD, the topic being globalisation and cricket. There was talk of following the England team on the next Ashes tour as research. It never happened. I completely ran out of academic steam and reverted to journalism. Football fanzines were well-established and gaining gravitas, with *When Saturday Comes* managing to take the leap towards the mainstream. If anything, the stereotypical cricket fan – old, male, slightly nerdy, obsessed with the trivial – seemed more suited than those packing the terraces each Saturday afternoon. And, of course, the game itself was much longer with numerous breaks. You needed reading material anyway.

So there I was, outside Lord's shouting like a market trader as the crowds poured out of the tube station and on to the streets. *JM96** was supposed to be intelligent, fun and humorous. So we made up patter to draw a crowd. The ones that stick in the mind are 'Guess the weight of Andy Moles and win a free subscription to *JM96**' and 'Nude pictures of Mike Gatting on page 3...4...5...6...7 and 8'. Pretty puerile stuff. The fanzine gathered steam and, a year later, even found some legitimacy in WHSmith's. However, after crossing the corporate Rubicon, the businessmen took over. Following talk of become 'the *Loaded* of cricket' *JM96** passed away quietly.

On that early September morning in 1993, a sizeable crowd had squeezed into Lord's so we found a pub to watch the game and count our sales. From their 60 overs, Sussex amassed 321/6, the biggest total the fixture had seen, especially given that late-season dew often caused a rattle of early wickets for the team batting first. At the innings break, we went home. We had done our job for the day and so, it seemed, had Sussex. I remember passing a smattering of disbelieving Warwickshire fans who were on their way home as we walked to the station. But the Bears were a doughty, innovative side in the mid-1990s, qualities personified in their captain Dermot Reeve. Roger Twose would hoist a shot over the infield to give Warwickshire the two runs they needed off the last ball. It was a staggering victory and quite the opposite of Somerset's today. Still, after a spate of runner-up positions it meant a lot to the West Country men, even though Lord's was far from sold out.

It cannot have helped that England were playing at the Ageas Bowl at the same time. A good proportion of the crowd at one-day finals were just cricket fans, neutrals who loved the game or another county. It is tempting to call these the 'cricket family' but that phrase has been stolen by corporate sport. Only governing bodies use it these days and when they do they actually mean sponsors, hangers-on and those who love the event, the food and the booze, more than the sport. They are easy to deride but those associated with them put their hands in their pockets and pay for the game. I would benefit from a World Cup freebie later on in the season, something that I truly appreciated. For me, as long as the corporate clients respect cricket, they are most welcome to their prawn sandwiches.

The game at Hampshire was a proper warm-up. The playing squads were fluid, some players would bat but not bowl and vice versa, so it was a game if not a true one. It would still draw a crowd of 11,000, only 5,000 less than the Lord's final. Australian batsmen David Warner and Steve Smith were playing their first games in England after serving bans for ball tampering. A Twitter debate broke out about whether they should be booed throughout the summer. It turns out they would but it tapered off dramatically, partly because Smith's batting in the series was worthy of so much respect while Warner's form was barely risible. The spectator who turned up at the Ageas Bowl in fancy dress as a huge cricket ball with a sandpaper hat was the highlight of the stick their pair received.

I started the day flicking between the two games but, as the afternoon wore on, I drifted. Friendly games at any level do not hold the attention for me, and neither do stale, controlled run-chases unless they are executed by Essex. I ran a Twitter poll on my county's best ever one-day final at Lord's. Surprisingly, the 2008 Friends Provident Trophy win over Kent finished on top, beating the 1979 Benson & Hedges Cup success, the club's first ever trophy some 103 years after their foundation. Maybe the result was merely down to the younger generation on Twitter. However, the 1979 win over Surrey broke a dam for the club in what has become known as the Fletcher-Gooch-Lever era and eight more trophies would arrive before 1986.

The 2008 game was less historic but it was against Kent, our derby rivals across the Thames. They posted a meagre 214 all out in the 50 overs but Essex were in trouble when Alastair Cook, batting at No 3, was out in the 24th over to leave them 93/4. However, an unlikely hero would complete the chase. Grant Flower was a most unassuming character and the accomplishments of his brother Andy always seemed to overshadow him, but Grant was a very capable all-round cricketer in his own right. His temperate 70* won Essex the 2008 Friends Provident Trophy Final and him the Man of the Match trophy.

Again, my canny knack of missing major Essex moments struck again but I remember regularly sneaking out of a big family party to get updates on the score. In fact, I have only seen Essex once in a Lord's showpiece game. I was fortunate to miss a debacle in the 1996 NatWest Final when Lancashire hit a paltry 186 then Essex were summarily dismissed for 57 in front of 28,000. My Lord's final saw Essex win but in highly unsatisfying circumstances. Captain Paul Prichard (92) and Nasser Hussain (88) starred in a first-innings score of 268/7 in the 1998 Benson & Hedges Cup Final. Then it rained. We huddled under the Edrich Stand for a few hours before eventually play was called off. On the reserve day, Essex bowled out Leicestershire for 76. We did not return and the trophy was held aloft in front of precious few fans.

Such tales of heroic failure and uncelebrated success would make the 2019 double all the sweeter.

Essex v Nottinghamshire (and the first impression)

Chelmsford, 15 May 2019

NOW, THIS felt much more like the cricket season. Spring had finally sprung, the temperature was rising but there would be more heat to come. The same could be said of Essex. Looking back at this game from a distance, the result had an inevitability about it. Nottinghamshire would suffer a terrible season ending in relegation, losing 10 of their 14 games. Before this visit, their last Championship win had come at Chelmsford almost a year earlier by a hefty 301 runs. There would be none in 2019 and, in the end, they mustered barely half the points of second-bottom Warwickshire. However, at this point, they had merely endured a tough start in the Championship and came into this game on the back of a Royal London Cup semi-final defeat to Somerset. The four-day game would be the domestic focus for the next two months and so Test players returned to the counties for Championship run-outs. That is why Stuart Broad was on duty for Nottinghamshire, his first-ever appearance in a four-day game at Chelmsford.

However, the opening day would belong to a player looking to push him out of the national side. Jamie Porter's 4-75 precipitated Nottinghamshire's dismissal for 187 on day one. He had followed his 75 wickets at an average of 16.82 in 2017 with 58 at 24.63 the following year. Porter had attracted the interest of the England Lions but a full cap never materialised when it seemed to be 'his time'. And, with the ever-tweaking rules of cricket, timing can be crucial. In their day one report, Cricinfo wrote: 'The seam of the Dukes ball is less pronounced this year, the heavy roller is back, and there are more matches in midsummer: three changes in one which mean the ECB will not be able to draw any worthwhile conclusions but which we can presume mean bowlers like Porter, with a pace not much above 80mph, will have their work cut out to maintain their standards.'

Porter's dismissal as a batsman would leave Essex 158/8 midway through day two and in danger of a first-innings deficit. However, Simon Harmer (43) and Peter Siddle (40) combined to add 81 in 23 highly entertaining overs. As the South African said afterwards it was one of those partnerships where they were sharp enough to hit the loose deliveries but not skilful enough to nick the good ones. It brought a joyous response from those of us in the Tom Pearce Stand to such an extent that we probably disturbed the office workers who had chosen to exploit the sunshine and take their lunch just a couple of hundred yards behind the ground on the banks of the River Can. One of the pleasures of visiting Chelmsford to watch cricket is the walk along the riverbank on a sunny summer day. The route from the members' car park in a field at the end of Meteor Way takes you past an 18-arch viaduct that dates back to the mid-19th century and a quite exquisite bridge. These are on the edge of what is called Central Park, an area made up of Bell Meadow and Sky Blue Pasture. It sounds part Pooh, Piglet, Eeyore and Tigger, part Rachel, Ross, Chandler and Monica. Much of this area has been rebuilt in my time supporting Essex. Fresh housing and a gym now occupy the area between New Writtle Street and the river. The stadium of Chelmsford City Football Club was situated on that site from 1922 to 1997. Then they sold up and lived a nomadic existence before laying down roots at the Melbourne Stadium on the other side of town.

When leaving the cricket ground via the river entrance and, after ducking through an unpleasant graffiti-strewn underpass, the path opens up to a much more pleasant scene. You can follow the Can into the centre of the shopping area. It is easily close enough to get there and back in the lunchtime break with provisions.

In June 2013, I went into the city, a status that Chelmsford had been given only 12 months before, with Lancashire nine wickets down and holding a lead of over 100 at the end of the first innings. I had some 'thinking work' to do for my job so I decided to take in a day of Division Two Championship cricket at Chelmsford to mull it over. Inspiration hit me as I took in my sandwich in the centre. Headphones on, head down, I beavered away. This task had been lingering for too long so, for once, I was content to miss the resumption. I was so engrossed that I lost track of the game for a while. When I finally saw the score, Essex were 11/5. I raced back to the ground to see the final overs of a memorable if horrible debacle unfold. Essex were dismissed for 20 in 14.2 overs over 68 minutes. Like Darren Stevens, Lancashire bowler Glen

Chapple was one of those players who haunted my side throughout the years. He had finished on an unbeaten 50 in the morning then, in the afternoon, recorded bowling figures 7.2-4-9-5. I took a picture of the scoreboard to remember my desolation. It would be the low point of the decade and the only time non-cricketing work colleagues would seek me out to discuss the County Championship score. Bad news always travels faster than good.

That pitiful 20 represented the lowest score in Essex history, some way short of the 30 they registered in 1901 at Leyton. Although it was only 30th in the list of lowest first-class scores, the overwhelming majority of these had taken place in the late 19th or early 20th century when pitches were uncovered and their upkeep was poor in comparison to today. The Lancashire game came almost 30 years to the day after Essex had dismissed Surrey for 14 at the same ground with Norbert Phillip (6-4) and Neil Foster (4-10) the destroyers. That was the lowest first-class score since 1907 and had tail-ender Sylvester Clarke not been dropped on 0 it may have been the smallest total in Championship history. The fast bowler slogged a four to not only put the team in double figures but, with that single shot, became the second-highest scorer.

Incredibly, the Surrey players contemplated drowning their sorrows at a local nightclub that night until one of their number pointed out they needed to follow on and bat out the game the following day, which they did. In one of those cricketing quirks, the game was drawn with both sides picking up the same number of bowling points.

Harmer collected four wickets as Nottinghamshire ended day two 90/6, a lead of 36. The South African had swung the game towards his side in emphatic fashion by precipitating the visitors' demise from 70/0 to 86/6 late in the day. His team would not let the game slip. Nottinghamshire were rolled over for 158 and Essex knocked off the requisite runs for the loss of two wickets.

By now, murmurs around The Hundred were as much a part of the conversational hubbub at Championship games as the weather. Details were gradually emerging and so was vehement dissent. During the Nottinghamshire match, *The Cricketer* magazine revealed the findings of their annual survey, which had drawn 900 responses. The Hundred was met with overwhelming disapproval; just six per cent indicated they were likely to go to a game. These readers could be considered hardcore supporters and the new tournament was designed to broaden the fanbase of the sport.

The *London Evening Standard* reported that the ECB's 100 million data points had shown 'those who attend cricket in the UK are overwhelmingly male (82 per cent), white (94 per cent), affluent (65 per cent ABC1) and have an average age of 50'. However, Surrey chief executive Richard Gould disputed the figures. The report added: 'Surrey's research of their Twenty20 sales over the last three years shows that one-third of attendees are between 25-34, the average age is 38 and only 18 per cent are over 55, one in five purchasers are women and family tickets made up more than 20 per cent of all tickets sold. This is clearly a smaller sample size than the ECB's figures, which encompass all men's professional cricket.' Gould said: 'There was frustration that the numbers used by the ECB seemed to be there to be critical of existing cricket and its fans in order to promote the idea for The Hundred.'

This sort of spikey ECB vs county dialogue was becoming prevalent now. It may have been borne of the initial roll-out.

'There was no consultation,' Gould would later tell the 2020 *Wisden Almanack*. 'The county CEOs were brought into a room, and told The Hundred was happening. It was released to the media ten minutes later, while we were still in the room. It was delivered as a fait accompli. The ECB then used all their leverage to make their dream become reality.'

The first impression

As you get older, your memory seems to act like a contour map. It only allows you to recall occasions that you saw fit to elevate to a certain level of importance at the time. However, the innocence of joy and novelty are gradually diminished by the years so monotony and repetition reduce the size of the spikes. This explains why you might clearly remember the colour of the train set you received at Christmas when you were six but cannot easily recall where you went on holiday two years ago.

With that it mind, it is revealing that my memory did not see fit to safely file away recollections of my first trip to Chelmsford. Our family were followers of cricket, if not regularly spectators at the Essex ground. I do remember patrolling outside of The Castle Park, Colchester and Valentine's Park in Ilford on Sunday afternoon drives. These often meandered away from our house for an hour and then back for another hour, the only point of the exercise that I could discern at the time was getting an ice cream. This was perfect for the five-year-old me. Later in life, I realised that getting boisterous children out of the house served as an important pressure-valve for fraught parents and, anyway, going for a Sunday drive was still a perfectly plausible weekend excursion in the 1970s and early 1980s.

At Ilford, I recall peaking through the window of our lime green Cortina, beyond a wrought-iron fence and a thicket of spectators to catch fleeting glimpses of men in white clothes. In retrospect, I should have thrown a trademark tantrum to go in as, alas, Essex would stop playing at Valentine's Park in 2002 and circumstances conspired that I never saw the team in action at this much-loved venue. Southchurch Park, Southend would follow suit a couple of years later and, though they decamped to Garon Park for a few years, Essex stopped playing by the seaside in 2011. The county finally gave up outground cricket entirely after the visit of Middlesex to Colchester in 2015.

In my youth, festival cricket was akin to the circus coming to town. Let's not be too romantic, the whole population did not attend and it did not dominate every conversation but these were meaningful annual occasions that attracted day-trippers to an area, which meant trade, attention and a certain level of excitement.

Essex were among the first counties to fully extract festival cricket from their schedule. The issues, so we were told, were economic. While these were hardly state of the art facilities, it was a sizeable operation to repurpose a public park for professional sport. Contributions from local authorities had eased the burden in decades gone by but the wind of town politics was changing and sometimes counties were left to fund 'cricket weeks' on their own. Contraction or extraction hit the fixture list.

The loss of outgrounds is among the first targets for curmudgeons seeking to attack the modern game. These were among the most cherished weeks of the county season as you were much closer to the players and the action in the middle. The more homely facilities of a large club ground were utilised. You could sit within a few yards of the players in the batting side watching from the pavilion and they would often wander about the ground in search of various detritus as the game went on; a bucket of ice from the pavilion, a helmet from the car. Occasionally they might spend 30 minutes in the public seats chatting with a friend or, in a slow passage of play, amble around the perimeter of the pitch to pass the time.

During a rare non-Essex excursion, I watched Indian legend Virender Sehwag, then of Leicestershire, hammer Middlesex to all parts of the delightful tree-lined Walker Ground on a gorgeous afternoon at Southgate. It was my closest county cricket venue at the time and even then the domestic game was a mental cleansing agent. An hour after his ferocious innings of 130, Sehwag strolled past me as I watched from the boundary rope nodding polite hellos and scribbling the odd autograph. How different this must have felt to the adulation he received back in India. My favourite festival story of all time came at the same ground in 2002 when Essex captain Ronnie Irani, exasperated at Middlesex skipper Andrew Strauss for failing to declare at lunch and provide a competitive chase on the final afternoon, ordered ice-creams for his side during the tea interval. Twelfth man Joe Grant wandered on with a box containing seven strawberry ices, four Cornettos and a choc-ice which the team lapped up sitting on the edge of the square.

The first Essex game that I can be sure I attended was at Harlow on 27 June 1982. I still remember walking across the pitch after the conclusion and running up the high banks around the boundary. The programme is still in my loft, I had bothered to keep it at the time and will never throw it away. It was in the John Player League, the much-loved 40-over competition that ran for four decades. It started in 1969, six years after the Gillette Cup, and gave added impetus to one-day cricket. Until 1991, all the games were played on Sundays and BBC television normally showed a weekly fixture. For those who did not attend games, the John Player League 'was' county cricket in the 1970s. Tests and cup games were shown during the day when many people were at work but these knockabout affairs on *Sunday Grandstand* might catch your attention if you were flicking through the channels. Mind you, that assumed your television had one of those new remote control things.

Like the early Twenty20 and perhaps The Hundred, the John Player was considered a sideshow in the early days. Thankfully, YouTube has preserved many of these games and their particular brand of late 20th-century English sporting charm. The crowd was normally a sedate sea of floppy white sun hats eating 99s. They sat in serene reverence watching well-known international stars and top-quality imported players vie with solid county sweats to become heroes of the afternoon. The likes of Gordon Greenidge, Waqar Younis and Courtney Walsh made up the first group while the middle set were often would-be South African internationals such as Clive Rice, Barry Richards and Mike Procter whose country of birth was in sporting isolation due to apartheid. However, in many ways, the final group were the most revered. These men sometimes did not look like cricketers or even sportsmen but many continued to be match-winners well into their 40s. They had been largely overlooked by international selectors but their hard-won combination of guts and guile consistently turned around seemingly impossible situations. Players like Brian Brain, Eddie Hemmings and Colin Milburn fit into this category. The closest Essex got was Stuart Turner, one of the best uncapped players in modern county cricket and a hero of many John Player League Sundays. But the archetype of this trope of idiosyncratic local hero-turned-national star was Colin Dredge. One of seven brothers from Frome, this lumbering fast-medium pace bowler was a stalwart of a spectacular Somerset side that included the likes of Ian Botham, Joel Garner and Viv Richards. His action was a feat of human engineering, an exaggerated lolloping stride towards the stumps culminating in a frantic gather and whippy delivery. It was once perfectly described as 'a pall-bearer fighting off a wasp'.

Another pair of Sunday afternoon mini-heroes were on show for Leicestershire at Harlow that afternoon. Les Taylor and Ken Higgs would both finish as top wicket-takers in a season of the John Player League. Jonathan Agnew and future Essex wicketkeeper Mike Garnham were also in the line-up for the visitors. Clearly, I had little appreciation of the game at that age as I remember nothing of the play but there was all manner of incident. Rain reduced the fixture to a 30-over affair then Essex were 28/5 before Norbert Phillip (44) and Turner (35) added 77 for the sixth wicket. The West Indian would also dominate with the ball, recording figures of 6-1-11-4 as Leicestershire mustered a mere 95 in pursuit of the home team's 114. Looking back these are truly pedestrian scores; modern Twenty20 teams look for double this tally from 50 per cent fewer deliveries. Of course, the pitch and conditions play a significant role, and perhaps this contributed to the club's decision never to return to Harlow. Given this was one of the post-war new towns and, in the 1980s, still possessed deep East End roots, it seemed a shame to cut off a potential avenue of reconnection. Especially as Leyton, the club's original ground had hosted its 407th and last first-class game in August 1977. However, back then, Ilford still represented an easy, pleasant opportunity for London-based supporters to catch the team.

In June 2019, Essex reaffirmed their connection with east London by opening a cricket hub on the site of their old ground at Leyton. The scheme, undertaken in conjunction with Waltham Forest council and the ECB, was part of the governing body's wider plan to connect with the south Asian population and get women playing cricket. This was the true grassroots of the game, putting on free events for disadvantaged groups, getting housewives involved and formalising children's tape-ball games. Essex are rightly proud of spearheading this venture but returning to play games in east London would be a step change.

In 2010, the club made public their interest in hosting Twenty20 games at the then 2012 Olympic Stadium. They would bid to become a joint-tenant of the venue. Reports in 2013 spoke of games in 2016, then in 2016, Essex chief executive Derek Bowden told the BBC: 'The objective is to play cricket there in 2018, probably play two or three home Twenty20 games in a two-week period.' The issue remains a regular question at members' meetings. It makes sense given the quality of the stadium, the ease of access and the connection with the stadium's current tenants, West Ham United. However, there are numerous road-blocks, not least of which is that the crowd Essex would be expected to draw might not make the event financially viable. In addition, the London Stadium, as it is now called, has been used for athletics events and concerts during previous summers and, even in the days of drop-in pitches for different events, the Hammers groundsmen may not welcome this sort of use for their pristine turf.

That said, let's ponder the future here. One of The Hundred's key arguments is that fans identify with cities more than counties these days. A fact that, handily enough, allowed them to concentrate their new franchises wholly on major population centres with Test grounds. They hope to invigorate new supporters by having teams playing right on their doorstep.

The population of London was due to reach nine million just before The Hundred was due to start in 2020 whereas other venues such as Leeds would be home for 830,000 people and Cardiff only 367,000. Therefore, if The Hundred proves successful, the most logical city for expansion would be London. Given the vast size of its population, it could easily accommodate a third franchise and the London Stadium would be an obvious venue in which to expand. The Oval covers the south of the city, the Lord's team attracts those from the north while the London Stadium would cover east London, a community that has been served by Essex in the recent past. You could argue that this is a southern or London bias but the ECB's own rationale suggests that they have targeted densely populated areas. If London added a third franchise that will mean it has one team for every three million people.

It is highly unlikely to happen. The Hundred was scheduled to run from mid-July to mid-August with its conclusion coming just before the Premier League season starts. No football club will take kindly to their preparations being hindered by a cricket tournament. Each franchise hosts only four home fixtures and drop-in pitch technology has advanced, so it is a burden one could envisage Tottenham Hotspur bearing in the years to come from an NFL team. The London Stadium transformed itself for another US sport in 2019 when it hosted four Major League Baseball games. But, remember, these were strategic implementations made by well-heeled American sports looking to gain a foothold into new markets. Forgive my cynicism, but the excuses would pour out to prevent the expansion of cricket in the same way, especially if it is not likely to be highly profitable.

Soon after selling their first ground Leyton in 1922, Essex became nomadic, taking the game all over the county, sometimes to different venues in the same town in the same year. The ground in Chelmsford was only purchased in 1966 and it would take another 50 years before it became the sole venue. Colchester was the last outpost to fall and it was cherished more than any other. My abiding memory of The Castle Park came in 2005 when Essex lifted the totesport League title, aka the old Sunday League. Ronnie Irani's side had bossed the competition from the start and victory over Hampshire on 28 August would allow them to lift the trophy with something to spare. It was a gorgeous summer day and I remember the venue, nestled in the shadow of old Roman

Garrison and alongside the River Colne, seemed to be shining.

In modern parlance, the fan experience was average for the time, just the usual ice-cream and burger vans and beer tents. Any temporary stands on offer did not extend far around the perimeter therefore most of the crowd were on chairs at ground level, with the outer rows elevated higher to allow them to peek above the heads of those in front. However, the setting and proximity to the players more than made up for that. Colchester was full to bursting that day despite the fact that the 2005 Ashes was gripping the nation, let alone the cricketing crowd, and the fourth Test at Trent Bridge was reaching its conclusion. Radio whispers about England's progress went around all day as Essex opener Will Jefferson bashed 88 as the home side reached 222 from their 45 overs. John Crawley and Nic Pothas put on 95 for the opening wicket in reply. But, as usual that year, the spin of Danish Kaneria stymied their assault after the fielding restrictions loosened. The Pakistani twirler would record 9-2-26-3 as Hampshire fell 12 runs short. Essex had won a trophy at an outground for the first and only time in their history.

The celebrations under the pavilion smacked of the old days of the Gillette and Benson & Hedges Cups when formal presentations were held on the players' balcony after each game. The squad had their own celebration too, a song that they had sung throughout the competition. It started with a player in the middle banging the end of a bat on the floor and recounted how the 'Eagles were going to shit on you' with gathering speed and volume. Their rendition after the Hampshire win was so loud it could be heard outside the pavilion. Rumour has it that the leader of this little ditty and chief bat thumper was Alastair Cook, then an up-and-coming opener but not a regular in that one-day side. The following week, Cook would hammer home his credentials with 214 in 238 deliveries against the Australians in a tour game at Chelmsford. The following March the 21-year-old would score an unbeaten 104 on his Test debut at Nagpur. He would be a fixture in the side until that incredible century-making farewell at The Oval in September 2018.

As it happens, the Australians at Chelmsford loom large in another of my earliest cricketing memories. Until researching this piece I thought it was my first game but, in fact, that fixture at Harlow was played the year before the 1983 World Cup. This was only the third time the competition had been played and, after this version, it would start to venture outside England. The opening two tournaments had featured eight teams and a total of 15 games played at six different venues. The 1983 version saw the first change in that format with eight teams playing 27 games at 15 venues, including relative backwaters like Tunbridge Wells, Worcester, Leicester, Derby, Swansea and Chelmsford.

One of my first cricket memories is watching Australia v India at the Essex ground. Again, I can recall precious little of the game but there is a firm recollection of being sat in that stand opposite the pavilion, now the Felsted School Stand, and watching the Australians warm up in the nets. After that it gets hazy as I clearly recall watching Dennis Lillee and Jeff Thomson go through their preparations but only the latter played in the game. However, his pace bowling partner was in the squad and played in four of their six games in the tournament so it is very possible that he was warming up too. The Australian side also featured Rodney Hogg, Rod Marsh, Geoff Lawson, Allan Border and Trevor Chappell. The Indians fielded future legends Sunil Gavaskar, Kapil Dev, Kris Srikkanth, Mohinder Amarnath and Madan Lal. The scorecard now informs me they were bowled out for 247 in 55.5 overs and Australia were rolled over for 129 from 38.2 in pursuit. It was the end of an abject tournament for David Hookes' side, which had started with defeat to minnows Zimbabwe. Although, to be fair, the Africans also had India 17/5 at Tunbridge Wells before Kapil Dev turned the tide with 175 not out off 138 balls, including an unbeaten stand of 126 for the ninth wicket.

Holders West Indies and India would qualify from their group and, after semi-final wins, this pair also contested the final. You could argue that this was one of the games that shaped modern cricket. Incredibly, underdogs India would manage to defend 183 all out with something to spare. That day the West Indies fielded arguably the greatest combined bowling attack in history (Malcolm Marshall, Joel Garner, Michael Holding, Andy Roberts) and perhaps the best batting top four (Gordon Greenidge, Desmond Haynes, Viv Richards, Clive Lloyd). But their chase never took off and they were dismissed for just 140 from 52 overs.

The surprise of the Indian victory in 1983 cannot be overstated in the development of modern cricket. According to Wikipedia: '[It] was a major turning point for Indian as well as world cricket. The win boosted the popularity of the game in India, which was until then restricted to the urban areas. It also increased the popularity of one-day cricket in India as well as in general. India began to take ODI cricket seriously after the World Cup win and soon emerged as one of the best teams in ODI cricket. Indian corporates started to take an interest in cricket too and began to sponsor many international tournaments, marking the start of the rise of India as the leading financial power in cricket.'

You could argue that game at Chelmsford in 1983 was an important domino in the change in Indian cricket, which would in turn shift the entire balance of power in the sport. Kapil Dev's side came to Essex that day in need of a heavy victory over Australia in order to qualify. There would be further critical 'dominos' in the semi-final and final but, researching it back, it seems my brain has retained a sunny, sepia-tinted recollection of this pivotal game – not only for my cricket life but, it seems, for the future development of the sport. I just wish I could remember more.

Essex v Kent
(and the power of story)
Chelmsford, 27 May 2019

SINCE HIS full-time return to the Essex fold, Alastair Cook's form had been solid if unspectacular. *The Cricketer* magazine was a little more scathing. A few weeks before this game, in an article called 'The curious case of Sir Alastair Cook and Essex' they noted: 'Few batsmen leave the middle in a jovial mood, but Cook is disconsolate rather than angry, resigned as opposed to infuriated.' In this, his 100th first-class game for Essex, the real 'Chef' would re-emerge.

Cricket's big show was upon us. The World Cup started on the day Essex completed another comprehensive victory at Chelmsford. The event was ever only on Cook's radar as a spectator. His last one-day international had come five years earlier. However, one could only feel for Joe Denly, who was playing his first game for his county since being omitted from the England squad. The Kent captain chose not to contest the toss and Essex batted. Cook would profit. He hit Denly for consecutive fours late in the final session to reach his first Championship hundred in two years and his 65th in first-class cricket. Then came the curious part. When Cook was on 125 and sharing a fourth-wicket stand of 130 with Ravi Bopara, he flicked the ball down the leg side and ambled a single. The batsmen then saw the possibility of two and accelerated. However, Sean Dickson had raced around behind the wicketkeeper from first slip to collect. His throw beat Cook's lunge. It was his first ever run-out for Essex in red-ball cricket and only the third in his long, record-breaking career. The home side would lose their last seven wickets for 38 but 313 was an impressive first-innings score at Chelmsford in 2019.

After dismissing Kent for 182, Essex declared on 206/7 with Cook top-scoring on 90. It was the fourth time he had hit a hundred and 90-odd in his career in a two-innings game; he had never achieved three figures in both. All this meant Kent had to score 338 in 90 overs on the final day. It was an unlikely target but rain had curtailed play the previous afternoon and the visitors had developed a dogged reputation after batting three long sessions to secure a draw against Surrey a week earlier. However, Simon Harmer is made for such occasions.

His modus operandi is now well-known. After a few overs of seam, the South African pitches camp at the River End. He wheels away, ball after ball, over after over, beguiling opposition batsmen with his ability to illicit not only significant spin but also sharp lift. By many accounts, his handshake is akin to being in the grip of a bunch of bananas. Long, strong digits enable this fingersmith to perform his sorcery with such unerring consistency. Harmer collected 8-98 in the second innings to provide match figures of 11-170. By the time Essex completed the victory late in the afternoon of 30 May he was the leading wicket-taker in the Championship with 29 scalps.

A couple of hours later at The Oval, Imran Tahir edged Ben Stokes to Joe Root to complete England's victory over South Africa. The World Cup was underway.

* * *

Tales of meaning and identity made me a sports fan, a desire to share them ushered me into sports journalism and, if you have got this far, stories are keeping you reading this book.

My aim is to wrap important messages about feelings and emotions within narratives surrounding England's national sport at a time when its very existence is in doubt. At the back of their minds, even the most avid county cricket fan fears tales from the past may be all we will have if the next decade plays out badly.

No one attends a cricket match in a vacuum. Even the splendid isolation I enjoy while watching Essex at Chelmsford involves some sort of connection, however tenuous. Fans will say that a season drifts away when 'there is nothing left to play for'. What they really mean is there is no chance of a significant story in the remaining fixtures. Of course, the contest between batsman and bowler still remains, all of the subtlety and sporting endeavour is present but, whatever happens, it will not mean anything.

It was a privilege to witness the exploits of Essex in 2017 and 2019. The long-awaited success, especially for that first title win, was so unexpected and joyous that a supporters' story should be told. The timing was perfect personally. It was the distraction I needed and I just had to tell someone. Unfortunately, no one else really cared so I decided to start writing it all down.

However, there is a danger in stories, especially those we tell ourselves. If you are not a clear and obvious victor then one tends to weave a narrative in which you are the hero or at least can claim some sort of moral superiority. Football fans are naturals at this re-positioning. A defeated team's supporters will loudly claim bad luck or refereeing incompetence/bias was the main reason for the defeat. If that does not work then they will shift their focus to the inequity of resources between the teams or even the relative lack of vocal support in relation to their success. If that fails then, in last resort, fans will mock their opponents for the close nature of the defeat. In practical terms, this last manoeuvre is from 'You only sing when you're winning' to 'How shit must you be, it's only 3-0'.

County cricket fans are guilty of the same process, albeit a more diluted and civilised version. There are the 'haves', who play on Test grounds, and have-nots, who do not. The success of the latter is over-celebrated while the trophies won by the former are derided. At this juncture, I should point out yet again that, on Twitter, I refer to Surrey CCC as '$urrey' and was quite happy to attempt to tear down their Championship success in 2018 by pointing out that one title in 16 years is utterly insufficient for a club of their abundant resources. As a fan, it was delightful to see Ryan ten Doeschate and Matt Quinn cling on during the last session of the final day amid a frisson of skullduggery to deny them the opportunity to match the unbeaten season of Essex the year before.

However, the fact remains that Surrey were the best team in 2018 and even the slights surrounding their past 'cheque-book' recruitment policy held little weight on this occasion. Still, there will be some that claim that it was not merited in some way. We are all emotional humans, liable to twist perceptions of reality to our own established narratives. This can be highly dangerous when your personal story changes as mine did in late 2016. I looked the same and acted the same but, in the eyes of the employment market, I was a different person. That's if they were even seeing me anymore.

I returned to the UK with no job and a bruised ego. It was not a healthy combination. My something-will-come-up attitude eroded during 2017. I received a wealth of loud, highly contradictory advice – 'take the first job that comes' to 'wait for the right gig' and from 'don't price yourself out' to 'be selective, be expensive'. Frankly, I did not know what to do. I applied for a specific group of relevant jobs, got interviews, sometimes had second calls but always missed out. On a few occasions, I was runner-up. This was disappointing but enough to sustain a personal story of success. For a start, I was close to victory having beaten a host of other applicants and, secondly, this process normally involved a candid and predominantly positive follow-up conversation with the interviewer.

Then I got an interview for an average level job at a very prestigious organisation. I travelled up the night before and stayed over in one of those cheap hotels characterised by easy-clean surfaces, inadequate curtains and paper-thin walls. I shivered through the first part of the night then woke up obscenely early due to a mixture of anxiety and early-morning sunlight. The interview was horrible. It was almost like a contest of faux-interest. My first impression of the place, the people and their attitude felt all wrong.

I believed the organisation was puffed up with self-importance. They may have thought precisely the same of me. My answers were OK at best but I still thought my background made me a strong candidate. However, one advantage of middle age is a greater understanding of what you are not. I resolved to call up the following morning to pull out of the process. But I neglected to contact them for a couple of days and I was a little taken back when I received an email saying thank you but they would not be taking the process forward. Again, reflection makes me think I wanted the validation of them being impressed enough with me before I could reject them. This sounds like narcissistic sixth-form dating nonsense but a lack of ego appeasement would colour my job applications during 2017.

A few months later, another role would emerge. On paper, this fitted perfectly and I diligently applied a day after it was advertised. This time, my questioner was someone I knew. He would be my boss, another prick to the ego given that we had been peers previously. As it transpired, the job was mundane with little room for development or expansion. Before the interview, I had been asked to wait on a set of sofas opposite the communal coffee machine. The office was on a basement floor lined with rough brown carpet and starkly illuminated by strip lighting. As I polished my mental notes, two office workers chatted conspiratorially as they made their cappuccinos and, within earshot, pilloried the performance of a mutual colleague. The bitching, the stifling environment and the narrowness of the job prompted me to pull out the next day. Looking back, it also protected my ego from another rejection. This job suited my skills and experience and it was with someone who knew me. Not getting it would have been crushing.

Not that I was idle in 2017. I managed to pick up some well-paid consultancy work on the other side of the world. Frequent trips made for exciting social media posts. Yet again, it was a harder yet more interesting route. But whom I was trying to impress was open to question. When that work ceased the following year I took more freelance gigs for much less money because they were interesting and allowed me to travel to a new country. Again, at this point, I must klaxon my good fortune. Bills were being paid, work was taxing yet hardly back-breaking and, through some hustling on my part, I was enjoying new experiences. Yet 2017 remains the worst year of my life.

On the surface, a story of success could be spun but the reality was different. Fortune had favoured me because I was reasonable at my job and had connections. But consultancy contracts do little for your security, financially or emotionally. Petty jealousies at roles I did not get or had not even known about would bite. Despite the shield of a lucrative short-term contract, it felt like others were moving on and leaving me behind. What would happen when that ended? This situation allows for more damaging stories to form. The ones you repeat in your mind to spark anger, paranoia and destructive bitterness. Through the grapevine, I heard that one person in a rival business was criticising me, personally and professionally, in order to retain a key contract. I had been asked by a mutual client to have 'a chat' then found out and a metaphorical knife was plunged in my back by someone who I had known for years. I do not know this for sure. It was floated by a well-placed friend as 'a possibility' then another respected colleague added that the miscreant had done the same to them. From that, I created a narrative of unethical behaviour on their part and a hero story of moral rectitude around myself. The accused had been found guilty in my own personal kangaroo court. Our paths have crossed since but I have deliberately avoided contact. This is taxing for me but, I venture, the accused thinks nothing of it.

Holding grudges is like drinking poison and expecting the other person to die. But, in my mind, the morals of this story were so clear it was impossible to let go. Working sporadically and with few close colleagues precludes the filter of differing opinions and the simple pressure valve of casual conversation. As 2017 went on and more jobs slipped by, I feared showing signs of desperation. Every email would be finished with 'and if you hear of anything do let me know' while recruiters stopped being interested if I did not bite at the first carrot they dangled. Coffees with former colleagues started to be cancelled and interviews became more infrequent. Then job descriptions written seemingly for me at organisations far smaller than those at which I had worked started to ignore my applications. I could handle not getting the jobs but, for a few of these, it seemed simply illogical not to be called for interview. When I chased up, apologetic recruiters would say they 'just wanted something else'. I felt I was being fobbed off.

Of course, all this prompts you to construct another set of protective stories: 'they are merely ageist', 'they are looking for the wrong qualities', 'the cult of the young has gone too far'. Then you turn the focus on yourself. If I had a different degree, had played the politics better, was younger or gone to public school my situation would be better. Probably the greatest lesson of all this is not to let your ego get in the way of personal progress. I still apply for jobs but now I assume nothing. Rejection after rejection has taught me to have zero expectation and that something was clearly wrong in a) what I was selling, b) what they were buying or c) a combination of both. Reskilling was a possibility but time was ticking. It would also cost money and mean starting towards the bottom. More importantly, I was already working in my main area of passion so I resolved to simply double down in my niche; work harder, smarter and try to evolve different skills. Even if that meant coping with the insecurity of freelancing.

Again, stories kick in once more. The facile projection of empty accomplishment is all too easy these days via personal social media and professional equivalents such as LinkedIn. Everyone must have a personal brand, even when it is crystal clear they have little to sell. It is a game I played but, in truth, this was nibbling around the margins. My psyche is ill-equipped for the self-promotion necessary to truly break through. However, that does not stop my anger at those self-marketers who, like Cockney market traders, spin attractive salesmanship to those passing by. We all know people who 'puff up' their CVs, claim credit for others' ideas and promote personal success using yardsticks that no-one can verify. However, when our elected political leaders were indulging in such shenanigans in public view then one must expect others to follow. If this was 'the game' these days then perhaps I was jealous that others were simply more skilled, confident and happy to bend the rules. Maybe it was just an excuse but I told myself I did not want to play.

Looking back on these three years is illuminating. Yet again, it is easy to paint a story of success in terms of money, career growth and, crucially for me, personal development in line with my values. If I really wanted to plod along, having my ego stroked and earning decent money, I could have done so for the past few years. But I have broadened my life by barging my way out of a comfort zone. The world tells us this is commendable, right? They do not make motivational posters of beautiful people running across stunning terrain backed with slogans like 'Play it Safe', 'Be fearful of failure' or 'I wouldn't do that if I was you'.

Instead, they tell us to 'seize the day', gamble and go for it. Well, I did that and I lost. Or at least I feel I did. Even then the world says you should pat yourself heartily on the back for your bravery, safe in the knowledge that you tried. Then, with chutzpah oozing from every pore, dust yourself down and 'go again'. But what if you are still bruised, what if you cannot face another rejection, what if you do not really know what you are doing and what if, deep down, you now fear you were never that good in the first place?

This is what faces a lot of people as they reach 50. Often that smooth ascent, in their career and life, has long-since flattened off and you believe the world has limited your options. If you miss out on a key job or your relationship breaks down and you cannot construct a self-convincing story of success then what do you do? Especially when your lifestyle expectations will be set, there may be debts or bills and people depend on you. Yet again, I must stress, this fundamental weight was not on my shoulders. Financially, I was fine. You could argue perversely that might have lessened the lack of identity from which I was suffering. I would have mixed cement on building sites and cleaned toilets in central London at 5am as I did as a student, if it meant feeding my family. But it did not. I had the luxury of choice. The problem was deciding on what to do and then convincing other people to pay me to do it. Ego was working against me, I did not know what I was anymore. But I knew I had to try and find some definition for the next 20 years of my working life.

There is a real danger of all this being dismissed as a person with considerable privileges bleating that they do not have as much as they used to and jealously looking at their peers wanting more. I can write another long-winded, spineless apology; however, I hope I have made my good fortune clear. All the issues I have faced do not register on Maslow's Hierarchy of Needs. However, that does not mean they are insignificant. While I claim no expertise in this area, it seems clear that suicide rates among my demographic, middle-aged men, are the highest of any section of the UK population. Should you have any concerns in this area then seek professional help or at least start by consulting the notes from the Opening Up charity and its associated links at the back of this book.

Numbers from the Office of National Statistics in the UK notes that 30- to 44-year-old men were the highest group of suicides through the 1990s and 2000s but 45- to 59-year-olds have taken over in the last decade. In 2018, The Samaritans reported 'in the UK, men are three times as likely to die by suicide than women' and that 'the highest suicide rate is among men aged 45-49'. In the same year, The American Foundation for the Prevention of Suicide wrote: 'The suicide rates were higher among adults ages 45 to 54 years (20.04 per 100,000) and 55-64 years (20.20 per 100,000), with the rate highest among adults ages 52-59 years (21.56 per 100,000). Younger groups have had consistently lower suicide rates than middle-aged and older adults.'

It is not straightforward economic deprivation that leads to a higher rate of suicide either. A 2012 paper from San Francisco Federal Reserve found that low-income inhabitants were much more likely to kill themselves if they lived in high-income areas. It argued the pressure to 'keep up with the Joneses' was an important factor. More broadly, it has been cited that suicide rates are relatively high among richer nations because of the so-called 'no-one left to blame' phenomenon, when your outward circumstances are positive but your inward monologue remains negative. Sadly, cricket and suicide have strong links. An entire book has been devoted to the subject and the author, David Frith, once calculated that UK players are 75 per cent more likely to take their lives than the general population.

Despite a daily dose of outward and inward negativity, this issue has never hit me. Still, we all need to be mindful of the stories we tell ourselves and the refuges we find when the noise gets too loud. For some, it is alcohol, betting, drugs or family-dividing affairs. For me, it was stolen sessions at Chelmsford when I should have been working.

However, there are benefits to being 50 years old and directionless. One of the most important is my relationship with my daughter. For years my son was my 'mini-me'. In his primary school years, he acted similarly to myself so I treated him in the way I would have wanted at his age. He has developed his own personality as he has grown older and I confidently predict he will become a fine man. When I was his age I was already displaying some of the neuroses that would manifest themselves later on in life when I leapt out of my comfort zone. He is popular, grounded, bright and kind. While our shared love for sport binds us, I fear I will be forever failing to work cricket into his heart. But that is the tiniest price to pay.

It was always harder with my daughter. Sport was my seven-day-a-week job for years so perhaps she did not 'get me'. I was 'silly Daddy' or 'smelly Daddy' or the Daddy at which you rolled your eyes and went to Mummy. Now, I feel she likes me. The change occurred over three years of school runs. The education options were limited on our return to the UK so our children ended up moving to a small primary school on the other side of our town. This meant a 30-minute round journey twice a day plus drop-off time. After the first year, it was just the two of us. Soon I managed to move beyond the stupid songs and cretinous jokes that every father hides behind to start having proper conversations. I found out what she liked to talk about and games she wanted to play. As we entered the third year, I started to get unsolicited hugs at home.

The drive itself was awful, a meandering slalom across a market town involving impatient jaywalkers, pushy drivers, Neanderthal teenagers, a kaleidoscope of traffic lights and enough sleeping policemen to ruin my suspension. She learnt several new swear words over the years as we rushed out of the house to avoid the ignominy of signing the dreaded 'late book'. I am writing this at the end of her last spring term before moving to secondary school. I will not be needed then. This is great news. Not least for watching Championship games. I used to arrive early after I raced to the ground after dropping her off but nearly always curtailed my afternoon session to pick her up. I rushed away from Chelmsford on the day Essex lifted the trophy for the first time in a generation in 2017 to take her to her first competitive netball game. All those school runs are a restriction for anyone but especially if you are trying to get a consultancy business off the ground and have a somewhat unhealthy obsession with county cricket.

Yet I am going to miss them terribly when they are gone. The congestion was ridiculous, the driving was needlessly aggressive and it was stressful managing my daily routine around pick-ups. But it was a privilege to have her undivided attention for so long every day.

Yorkshire v Essex (and what are we really angry about?)

Headingley, 3 June 2019

WHEN ESSEX visited Yorkshire at the start of June, Somerset had just gone 15 points clear of Hampshire at the top of the County Championship table. As a result, this fixture felt like a play-off for the right to join the title fight.

Meanwhile, the early stages of the World Cup had served to support the pre-tournament expectations. The only modest surprise came on the eve of the Essex trip to Headingley when Bangladesh bashed 330 at The Oval to beat South Africa. The following day, there would be the first proper jolt when favourites England lost to Pakistan by 14 runs. Headingley was to hold its first game in the tournament on 21 June. It would be the hosts' next defeat when they were dismissed for 212 in pursuit of Sri Lanka's 232. That result was perhaps the lowest point of the tournament for the eventual winners; even some late-order batting heroics from Ben Stokes could not save them on this occasion.

That was all in the future. The new Emerald Stand, all £43m of it, lay empty and waiting as Yorkshire amassed a sizeable first innings score against Essex on the opening day of an overlooked yet important game en route to the title. They bulldozered 224/2 at tea but persistent bowling from the visitors saw the hosts lose four wickets for 28 runs in 13 overs during the final session.

Will Buttleman was behind the stumps for this game. First-choice wicketkeeper Adam Wheater was still out with an injured thumb collected on the opening day of the season and loanee Rob White had damaged an ankle in training. Regular second XI gloveman Michael Pepper hurt his finger against Kent last time out so Essex were forced to give a full first-class debut to a 19-year-old who received the news while eating his Sunday lunch the day after scoring a century in club cricket. The misfortune of Essex wicketkeepers at the start of the 2019 season was freakish, prompting the peerless David Hopps to conclude his day one report at Headingley by quipping: 'They said it would be difficult replacing James Foster, but nobody said it would be downright dangerous.'

This would be the only Championship road game I would not attend. I toyed with the idea but the first day was not practical and the others were forecast for rain at one point or another. There was no option to stay over so an 'early morning out, mid-evening back' train journey seemed rather excessive for the privilege of watching the rain fall. In hindsight, I wish I had gone. It would have been long, mostly dull and expensive but one passage of play became an unsung highlight of the season.

On the second day, Yorkshire were bowled out for 390 and then reduced the visitors to 18/1 before rain ended play at 2.15pm. The latter half of the home side's innings was held together by 91* from Dom Bess, an off-spinner on loan from Somerset. His appearance in the Yorkshire side was a modern cricketing parable. Having burst into the Somerset side in 2016, 5-43 from Bess would put his side briefly top of the table in the three-way tussle for the title in the final round of fixtures that year. He and Jack Leach formed a formidable pair at Taunton on a helpful surface that was dubbed Ciderabad, one of the better puns from a seemingly infinite list down in the West Country. New national selector Ed Smith championed Bess, who was elevated to the full Test team in 2018. He did not shine and was jettisoned after two games. Since then Leach had assumed the main spinner's role at Somerset and so Bess was loaned to Yorkshire, who had been lacking a frontline slow bowler since Adil Rashid decided to concentrate on white-ball cricket. His relationship appeared to be complicated with Yorkshire and details are unnecessary for this story; suffice to say Rashid's choice was far from unique yet still a blow to the credibility of the County Championship. But far worse was to come when England selected him for a Test match against India in 2018 despite having not played a four-day game in 11 months.

I diverted towards this tale merely to point out that other sports simply do not act this way. Perhaps it was a product of the traditional strength yet modern weakness of the county game and the all-important position of the international team. Yet the latter was always dependent on the Championship for players. Certainly few sports would see a recent national team player being loaned to a direct title rival at a pivotal point in the season. Some Essex fans grumbled about their side having to face Bess but, at this point, Yorkshire were also a significant rival to favourites Somerset, who were bidding to put daylight between themselves and the chasing pack.

Back at Headingley, Bess would return 3-45 in the Essex first innings, the best figures among the Yorkshire bowlers. The visitors slumped from 190/3 to 191/6 in 21 balls. Buttleman's innings, a 37-ball duck, was indicative of the attitude after that. More rain was forecast but if they failed to avoid the follow-on, Essex would struggle to survive in this crucial game. It was going to be tight. The home crowd howled in protest when the umpires called the players off for bad light with 22 overs left in day two and Essex 19 runs adrift with two wickets remaining. This was nip-and-tuck cricket with the teams in and out for light, Yorkshire captain Steve Patterson delayed taking the new ball and, when he finally did, he bowled himself not Duanne Olivier, who was appreciably quicker and had hit Tom Westley on the head earlier in the innings. The fear was that the pace of the South African bowler against tail-enders would prompt the umpires into curtailing play in the gloomy conditions. These tactics seemed to have paid off when Patterson had Porter caught at slip. Number 11 Sam Cook joined Peter Siddle at the crease with 18 still needed to avoid the follow-on. If either were out, Essex were likely to lose.

The Australian took the lead in the partnership and was 39 not out at the close on day three as Essex finished on 252/9 after blasting past the follow-on total with a pair of sixes. The next morning they would see off any chance of a Yorkshire win by scoring freely for a further 70 minutes. Their last-wicket stand had added 86 in 25 overs. Siddle's 60 was his best score for Essex; Sam Cook's 37 was a career-high. The stand will not figure in too many lists for 'Highlight of the Season' but had this pair capitulated, the title race would have been a three-horse affair with Essex a few furlongs behind. It also smacked of the character of the team. As in 2017, someone, somewhere always stepped up. Siddle's spell at the club would be curtailed by an Ashes call, at which point he became the enemy of course. His return with the ball did not have the stellar statistics of Harmer but 34 wickets from eight Championship games in 2019 is still an excellent return, especially at an average of 20.08. In that single innings at Headingley he gathered more than a quarter of his total in all 11 innings with the bat during 2019. That tail-end cameo told Essex fans a lot about his character.

While never being one for inane bar-room banter, it was delicious that this mighty wagging of the Essex tail came at Headingley. The Yorkshire crowd hold a special place in their hearts for cricketing folk from my county, and not in a good way. It developed after Keith Fletcher was chosen above local star Phil Sharpe for the fourth Test against Australia in July 1968. The Yorkshireman had been called away from his county's game, ironically against Essex at Westcliff, to become the 14th man in an England squad struggling with a fresh injury to Tom Graveney on top of Colin Cowdrey's absence. Graveney would recover to captain the side and so Fletcher, already in the squad, made his debut. The Yorkshire crowd perceived the Essex player had snatched away a fairy-tale return for 'their man'. Sharpe was known as an excellent slip and outfielder so the groans started when Fletcher shelled several chances early on. Then he was out for a duck. The boisterous and highly vocal nature of both sets of supporters may have contributed to the lasting though hardly deep-rooted enmity between the counties. Still, the Western Terrace retains a raucous reputation and my first experience of it would be perhaps my most memorable day of international cricket. The highlight would be one of the greatest innings in Test match history. It would come from an Essex legend, aided and abetted by a county team-mate.

I cannot name the subject, I cannot name the building but I distinctly remember the feeling of emerging blinking into sunlight around lunchtime after my final exam at Newcastle University in June 1991. Like everyone else, I had been an academic hermit for a few months, trying all sorts of tactics to browbeat information into my brain before releasing it on to paper inside dimly-lit exam halls. Finally, it was over. University – the big goal, the life-changer, the pivot between school and work, childhood and adulthood – was done. Before questions such as 'what the hell am I going to do now' entered my head, I was going to celebrate. My flat-mate hailed from Leeds and invited me 'back home' as our exam schedule had coincided. The weekend plan was clear: alcohol, nightclub, alcohol, sleep, golf, alcohol, cricket, alcohol. He was not a close friend in any way; we had bonded as we bunkered down revising at home in our final days at university and other pals started to drift away from each other with an eye on their futures. Quite understandably, I can not remember much about the alcohol we drank but I do remember the golf on the Saturday afternoon. Another mutual friend – blond-haired, chewed his tees, that's all I recall – joined us as we hacked our way around 18 holes. It was the first time I had played on anything approaching a proper course. Someone had once told me that golf and cricket did not mix due to the need to pivot the back foot in the former and the fundamental problems with that in the latter. This, coupled with my general ineptitude, kept me away from the game. Still, it was the opportunity to thump a tee-shot down a long fairway with a beefy driver so I took my chance with both hands. They taught me the rudiments of tee-position and then I learnt the stuffiness of the sport as we were told off in the clubhouse for our attire. All this was the prelude to the Sunday when I would get to see a peak West Indian side play in the first Test at Headingley. My Essex hero, Graham Gooch, was 82 not out overnight. His county team-mate Derek Pringle was with him on 10. For all the 'good old days' reminisces of cricket in yesteryear, there was no issue with tickets. I think we just paid on the door. Gooch had earned enough respect throughout his career to quieten down even a Yorkshire crowd but his partner received sustained abuse. It was inevitable – he was a Cambridge-educated, earring-wearing, Essex all-rounder with an alternative streak. He was perceived as an underperformer on the international stage despite being afforded numerous chances. However, Pringle's 27, compiled in 94 balls over almost two and a half hours, would be critical to England's victory. The pair put on 98 for the seventh wicket. Gooch would carry his bat throughout the innings finishing on 154 not out, combatting Malcolm Marshall, Curtly Ambrose, Courtney Walsh and Patrick Patterson at the height of their powers in gloomy conditions. On the Saturday evening with England on 137/6, the umpires had offered the light to Gooch. He refused. Reports later suggested this was a psychological ploy to intimidate the bowlers.

His innings of 331 balls over 452 minutes would set up England for their first home victory in a Test against the West Indies since 1969, the year I was born. Pringle's 27 was matched by Mark Ramprakash but no other English batsman reached double figures. Gooch had scored 61 per cent of his team's runs and *Wisden* would rate the innings as the third greatest of the 20th century. The PWC Test rankings was later set up to order the best batting and bowling contributions assessing factors such as the conditions and the relative strength of respective teams. Gooch's effort was its highest-scoring innings.

The day ended with the West Indies 11/1. Phil Simmons had played on from a delivery by Phil de Freitas from the very first ball. The crowd built up to a mighty, soaring 'wooooaaahhhhh' as the England all-rounder raced in for the opening delivery then erupted at Simmons' dismissal. It is the only time I can remember seeing a wicket from the first ball of an innings in a red-ball game. It is a shame that I do not recall more of this game. It was such a pivotal game for England and I saw a classic contribution from the greatest Essex player I have ever seen. Yes, there are snapshots that remain in my memory but they are frustratingly few. Perhaps the history that would hang on this game was not really apparent at the time, or I was just too wrapped up in myself at that point in life. I had achieved an ambition putting letters after my name. This was a time when degrees were not so common and there existed a clear demarcation between a university, a polytechnic and a college of higher education. This is not to suggest the modern versions are not so valuable but, back then, my BA Hons certainly seemed that bit more exclusive.

Also, I was probably drunk on my own potential. Everything was possible, now it was just a matter of making my future. It was the moment in time that Hollywood constantly makes movies about, that period when you believe you have to make crucial decisions about your life but, looking back, they were far too seismic to take on and you were nowhere near qualified to consider.

University had made me someone different. Before I fell into the right crowd in my sixth form, I was destined for a bland career commuting into London from a bland Essex town. Who knows, it may have been a much happier life but, for certain, it would have been narrow. Ever since my student days, I have pushed back in situations where I felt my growth would be stifled. It is one of the few traits I like about myself, even those it has caused considerable angst to myself and those around me.

Looking back on that afternoon almost 30 years ago, I cannot remember Gooch sumptuously driving a forlorn Marshall down the ground for four or pulling Walsh to the square leg boundary to complete his century. I had to rely on YouTube and online reports for research. However, I do remember one remark from my flat-mate, a proper Yorkshire lad with whom I would entirely lose contact within weeks of that day at Headingley.

Deep into the final session, the Western Terrace was drunk. We were sitting in the front few rows and, to our left, one inebriated twentysomething was hurling abuse at something going on in the middle. Pint in one hand, cigarette in the other, 'Boris Johnson-hair' and his shirt partially untucked, he held court on the concourse spewing vitriol from his reddening face.

My flat-mate leaned over to me and said: 'Look at him. Pissed, loud and angry for no reason. That could have been me.'

But for university, it might have been me too.

Bikes at Fenner's for the game against Cambridge University in March, 2019

Essex take the field at Hampshire for the first time in the 2019 County Championship season

Hampshire on the opening day of the 2019 season

The view from the top of the pavilion at The Oval on day two against Surrey with the London cityscape in the background

The lunch interval at The Oval

County cricket may be the only sport that encourages kids on the field to play the game in the interval. Long may it continue

How Nottinghamshire use the greatest English fear, embarrassment, to stop movement behind the bowler's arm

TRENT BRIDGE
EST 1838

STOP

PLEASE DO NOT MOVE WHEN THE BOWLER IS BOWLING FROM THIS END OR YOU WILL DISTRACT THE BATSMAN, INTERRUPT THE GAME AND BE VERY EMBARRASSED!

Proof: No one watches county cricket

The spot at Chelmsford where my father and I used to watch Essex

Sunshine over Edgbaston but rain clouds over Birmingham in the background

A double rainbow at Canterbury on my 50th birthday

Another great part of Championship cricket is being able to inspect the wicket. This is Trent Bridge

Alone together, three men watch Essex

Essex CCC named its pavilion after one of its greatest servants in 2017

The final overs of the day/night game against Middlesex in 2017. Simon Harmer picked up the final wicket just before 9pm

The three teams on the field. Surrey batting, Essex in the huddle and the umpires making preparations. This was during the last home game of the season

The original purchase of the ground at Chelmsford in 1966 was only possible because of an interest-free loan of £15,000 from the Warwickshire Supporters' Association. This would have a value of £238,000 in 2020's economy

My view for finals day in the Vitality Blast at Edgbaston

The Essex players celebrate with the fans after winning the Vitality Blast for the first time in their history

Rain clouds over Taunton in the Championship decider. There was no play at all on day three

Essex v Hampshire (and living life like you play cricket)

Chelmsford, 16 June 2019

THIS WAS the fifth game Essex would play in the Championship, one behind everyone else bar relegation-threatened Warwickshire. Even allowing for the stagger to unwind, the table looked daunting. Ten Doeschate's men came into this game lying fourth with 65 points, 10 shy of Yorkshire, 20 adrift of Hampshire and a full 50 points behind a Somerset side who had drawn just one match and won the rest.

The Championship season was only 35 per cent complete but the clock was ticking for Essex in the title race. They had to make a move and the time was now as they would be entertaining the top two in the next 11 days. Given all that, it was surprising to see overseas bowler Peter Siddle rested. Not dropped, not injured, but omitted with a view to his workload and the challenges ahead. This was odd purely because, on such occasions, it is normally easier for sports teams to present an opaque cover story like a virus, strain or 'niggle'.

Between the home fixtures with Hampshire and Somerset, I had to fly to Poland for a wedding. My flight was on Thursday so the plan was to stack up my emails, meetings and can-I-have-a-job-please coffees on Monday when there was rain around. That would free up Tuesday and possibly Wednesday to concentrate on this game. On the first day, there was also the little matter of India v Pakistan in the World Cup at Old Trafford.

At the start of 2019, Indian batsman Ajinkya Rahane might have still harboured hopes of playing in that fixture, one probably best measured on the Richter Scale. The last of his 90 one-day international appearances had come the previous February but a strike-rate of 78.63 seemed pedestrian these days. Still, with form and injury always fickle, professionals have to assume there is a chance. While I have never met Rahane and have no handle on his character it seems eminently possible he could have been weighed down by 'what ifs' on this of all days when the world was watching India. How did he handle his omission? Did he feel his career was sliding? What was the overriding emotion – anger, bitterness, resignation, relief or a determination? As Cricinfo pointed out, on the Saturday before the game he had told his 5.4 million Twitter followers: 'For positivity in life, you need to have a positive mind!' What was he feeling on this particular day, in front of a thousand or so at Chelmsford with the booming music from the Essex Pride festival drifting over from Central Park, when he might have been playing in a seismic encounter that received 700,000 ticket requests and had an estimated television audience of 1 billion. And, most pertinently, did all this contribute to his second ball duck on the opening morning and his first-baller in the second innings? My own loss of status had given me a few 'bad days at the office' over the years but thank heavens no one was scrutinising me in this way.

Rahane's dismissal was Porter's second in his opening 13 balls after a rain-delayed start. In the following over Sam Cook would have Tom Alsop caught to leave Hampshire 8/3. Although Sam Northeast and Rilee Rossouw rallied until lunch, Simon Harmer dismissed them both soon after the restart as the visitors subsided to 70/5 then 118 all out. The South African finished with 5-23. It was becoming a standard statistic for him.

Essex were 147/3 at the close and utterly in control with batting to come so, on the Monday morning, I stayed with my plan to attend on Tuesday. However, they would lose seven wickets for 67 runs before lunch on Monday with Kyle Abbott taking 4-54 including identical leg-cutters just four balls apart to trap Adam Wheater and Simon Harmer in front.

The deficit was only 96 but Hampshire rarely looked like reaching parity after they slumped to 16/4. Porter had Alsop lbw from the fifth ball of his second over to signal lunch. On the resumption, he immediately enticed Rahane to edge behind with his sixth. Sam Cook hobbled off so Harmer was introduced in the fourth over. In the sixth, he induced Northeast down the pitch and Wheater executed the stumping. Two balls later, Rossouw's agricultural heave was edged to Beard. Hampshire had been missing James Vince and Liam Dawson to England duty but, as their team manager pointed out afterwards, their own culpability was clear. Their two innings lasted less than 64 overs and Weatherley carried his bat in the second innings with just 29, the lowest total with which anyone had achieved that feat in Hampshire's history.

In the final over, Harmer pitched the ball outside off stump and got it to jag back towards the wicket. Mason Crane thrust his bat down and feathered an inside edge. It bounced off the body of the startled Wheater and the wicketkeeper instinctively thrust out a leg to volley the ball down the pitch. It flew up nicely for ten Doeschate to pouch a simple if bizarre catch running from short leg. Four balls later, Harmer ended the affair by snaring Fidel Edwards lbw.

Afterwards, the *Guardian* was prophetic. 'Somerset really can do no wrong! With a week off to contemplate their view from the summit of Division One, they must have been delighted with the news from Chelmsford, where Hampshire, their closest pursuers, were bowled out twice in 64 overs to lose by an innings in a day and a half. The only downside for the runaway leaders is that Simon Harmer's 12 wickets took Essex into third place, albeit 30 points adrift, but the 2017 champions know what it takes to get over the line. Next week's match between the two form sides may shape the second half of the season.'

The wedding was lovely, lively and thoroughly soaked in Polish vodka. Having long since left behind the rash of ceremonies you attend in your 30s, this was a relative rarity. I was a work friend of the groom and hardly knew anyone else, therefore it would muster up most of my social acumen not to be a sad solo among the party. Most of the non-family guests were younger and so being the sad, solo, older member of the party would have been worse. The phrase 'when did you stop dancing?' always comes back to me at weddings. For a while, I actually thought it was about that pivotal moment when at a social function, you realised your boogying had crossed the crucial line between expressive and embarrassing.

Actually, it is one of four famous questions a shaman might ask a tribesperson if they came to him complaining about being disheartened, disillusioned, dispirited or depressed. The others are: When did you stop singing? When did you stop being enchanted by stories? When did you stop finding comfort in the sweet territory of silence? Supposedly, these four activities are 'healing salves' and the cessation of any would lead to a loss of soul.

For the record, I did not dance at the wedding. I had given up all that nonsense around 2005.

'You play your cricket the way you live your life'

It was a throwaway remark by Shane Warne that I heard on television many years ago but it always stuck with me.

Many people, much more eloquent than I, have written about sport as a simile for the human condition. Most often we talk about the life lessons we can gain from team games – co-operation, communication and working towards long-term shared goals. At grassroots participation level, there is something in it. But in modern, professional sport, you tend to see less virtuous and admirable behaviour the more money is on the table. Football is the world's most popular game but the conduct of its most expert practitioners, along with those who coach and support them, is often deplorable. When you are young this does not tend to bother you but, as you get older, their manner starts to feel like another reason why the relative civility of county cricket should be cherished all the more.

We need to be realistic – this is all a vast generalisation. There are many noble and gracious people associated with football and some reprobates in cricket with whom you would not want to share slip duty. Also, we have to consider that money makes good people act badly and, yes, there is a class distinction between the games. Yet again, this is not about judgment, just difference. But, having played a similarly poor standard of cricket and football, I would much prefer to spend my time with team-mates from the former. Then again, my own experience suggests perhaps it was not about the people but the sport.

In my late 20s, I played Sunday league football in north London. This was a pretty horrible standard on pretty horrible pitches against some pretty horrible opponents. But, at that age and with my lack of ability, it was the only option if you wanted to play the traditional XI-a-side game. I was short, slow and hardly skilful but my knowledge of the game and speed of thought allowed me to hold down a place in central midfield. This was combative, elbows-out football. You had to stand up for yourself as they would literally stamp all over you when the ref was not looking. It was full of wind-up merchants, shirt-pullers and thugs who spent 90 minutes playing the man not the ball. I was none of those but, to my shame, I was prepared to dispute any decision and pressurise referees and, if possible, bend the rules my way. I would harangue the official over close decisions that might be 70:30 against my team, let alone a 50:50. If, heaven forbid, the referee made an incorrect decision against my side then I would remind him for the remainder of the game.

To put it another way, I was gobby with the capacity to be sneaky.

As it happened, my football club ran a cricket team. It was started by 'old boys' from the Sunday morning outfit as a means to carry on their sporting endeavours for a few more decades. In April/May and August/September, the football and cricket seasons would overlap so, on weekends when my body and the schedule could stand it, I would shuffle around the midfield for 90 minutes in the morning before keeping wicket in the afternoon. It was the same club and the same me, even some of the same people as a few of us doubled up. But I behaved in an entirely different way.

Yes, I was competitive and audible behind the stumps but this could be described as 'chirpy' not 'gobby', an important difference. As a wicketkeeper, it was my job to lead the appeals and I took to the role with gusto. But if the umpire made an error or turned me down then all he would get would be a few 'tuts'. If he gave me out while batting then I would go and if I knew I was out I'd walk. More often than not the umpire would be a member of my team and, yes, if I perceived that he had made a mistake giving me out then there may be a glare, small remark or body language in his direction that breached some ICC code. But this was rare. In the Sunday afternoon, friendly cricket that I played for decades I can only recall these heated exchanges happening on a handful of occasions. With football, it was weekly. Looking back, it is clear the culture of the sport determined my behaviour even when I was playing for the same club on the same day.

But Warne's comment also resonated in another way. My batting technique was always solid. As a junior, my club sent me to the Essex Cricket School for training. On the day, I found my skills behind many of the other boys. However, I was one of the best in my school and often praised for 'playing with a straight bat'. This time-honoured cricketing quality marked me down as an opener early on. I took to this role in my school years and early junior cricket as I got sufficient runs. I also possessed more patience and obduracy than most teenagers. Seeing off the opening and, probably best, bowler is a key skill but, after that, you need to score, especially in the men's Sunday cricket that I played as a teenager. If you were out as soon as you started to accelerate then the scorebook suggested you were just wasting time. This happened too often, and as a result, I went into my shell. I even requested to bat at No 11 for a while. I could spin the ball and, as a left-handed bowler, had offered a little variation in youth cricket. But, yet again, my sporting temperament let me down. I just could not handle being carted all over the ground, a fate that every bowler will suffer and a junior spinner will have to endure more often than most. The son of Essex all-rounder Stuart Turner sent me to all corners in a youth game and, in truth, I am not sure my bowling ever recovered.

Wicketkeeping seemed a decent alternative and placed you at the centre of the game. I found I was pretty good at it, more than adequate for the league cricket I played in Sussex and Hampshire in my 20s. However, for me, wicketkeeping was something to pass the time before I batted. That was the point of playing. Yet, as I got older, I began to tense up. At the end of my time, I dreaded batting or even turning out on a Sunday. Quite why I felt any pressure in these knockabout games I do not know. But the number of 30-minute, single-figure scores I endured does not reflect the semi-decent club cricketer I could have been. Certainly, a more laissez-faire view of my own endeavours would have given me more enjoyment.

I batted with a refusal to take real risk. I liked to think I was looking for the percentage shot but, in truth, I got more timid and fearful as I got older. Ditto this for real life too, with some notable exceptions. I could handle pressure, regularly fending off bouncers, close fielders and the odd sledge, but I had an unfortunate capacity to effectively get out to the ball before the one that got me out. A huge let-off or an unusual event would spook me and I would over-react mentally. I was hit on the heart by a sharply rising ball in a league game in Hampshire and struggled for breath for a few minutes. I refused to go off but fell to the oldest trick in the book, the yorker, a ball later. On numerous occasions, I would withstand a huge appeal or come close to being dismissed from one ball, only to somehow contrive to get out the next. This ability to over-react has also followed me in real life, though the last few years has led to a reasonable improvement.

Essentially, cricket is an individual sport within a team context. Batsmen and bowlers take the stage solo, although there are ten others in your supporting cast and you have to spend your fair share of the game out of the spotlight. Their success and failure is largely but not wholly dependent on their own efforts. This is why so many post-match conversations in the bar after club games are essentially self-centred dialogues disguised as two-way discourse. Everyone wants to talk about their own part in the game and gauge other's opinions. But that other party is themselves wrapped in their own contribution too. It always made for stilted conversation. There is probably a *Two Ronnies* sketch in the way team-mates steer their beery chats towards their own tale of heroism.

Not that I revelled in the social side of the game. Again, reflecting life, I became less social as the years went on. Once I had 'done my bit' in putting the sight screens away or collecting the boundary flags I'd be looking to shower, change and leave.

My retirement from playing cricket came in my mid-30s. By this time, I was married with a job that involved constant weekend work. When my first child came along it seemed selfish to spend most of my only day off playing a game I had ceased to really enjoy. My wicketkeeping was good but I was far from the batsman I wanted to be. Too slow, too ponderous but, let us be honest, probably just not good enough. I was holding myself up in comparison to the player I might have been. The teenager with potential, the one with a decent eye and a solid defensive game. It is stupid to think back on it now but I was starting to hope for rain on Sundays so my games were cancelled.

I picked up the team's scorebook at the end of one game and saw, alongside my pitiful one-figure total, that someone had scrawled 'IN 30 MINUTES'. Again, perhaps it is oversensitivity, but I made my excuses and left in silence at the end of the game.

It just so happened that my father died at around the same time and, in my mind, I linked the two events. He was the only person who seemed bothered whether I played cricket or not. Arthritis had ended his playing days early and so he had always advised me to keep putting on my whites for as long as I could. But this infuriating game continually exposed personal frailties in a way I did not like. I could not just enjoy it for itself, I had invested too much of my sporting ambition in being a competent cricketer. That was just not working any more.

So, in direct opposition to his wishes, after that game, I never picked up a bat again.

Essex v Somerset
(and The Grumbler)

Chelmsford, 24-25 June 2019

IT WAS only a few days past the summer solstice and the evenings were shortening imperceptibly but this still felt like a six-pointer. Somerset were still 30 points ahead at the start of play but a solid home victory could whittle that down to single figures. Given the gap had been 50 points a few weeks earlier, Essex fans felt like momentum was building and the importance of that final fixture at Taunton was already being discussed. It seemed that these two teams were going to race for the title and there was every chance that neither would have their noses far in front by then.

In my mind, there has always been a slender but significant link between these two counties. Primarily it was because they vied for the title of the biggest county outside of the Test grounds. Unlike the major clubs, they tended to grow their own players rather than pilfer the best from those around them. Over time, this had created legends with a real connection. As at Chelmsford,

Taunton's favourite sporting sons wear white. These were cricketing bolt-holes where the most important sporting events used a small red leather ball rather than a larger inflated one. Both teams had locations in the centre of their city or town, only a few minutes' walk from the main train station. Perhaps this helped cricket become more visible and important in the community. This might be manifested in training sessions for children, key groups and all the other fine work the club took on. But it was also significant that spectators could pop into town during lunch breaks. You were not imprisoned in the confines of the ground between 11am and 6pm so those in the city centre would become accustomed to lanyards swinging from members' necks and hats with three seaxes on them. These little prompts let everyone know there was a professional cricket club playing in Chelmsford. It also lifted the spectacle on Twenty20 nights. The atmosphere in any sporting event was always better in an 8,000-capacity ground full to bursting than a 25,000 venue that was only half-full. After a big-hitting Friday night fiesta much of that crowd would disperse into nearby bars and restaurants to celebrate or commiserate.

Then there was 1979. A full 40 summers ago Essex and Somerset shared all four domestic trophies, the first silverware for either outfit. It was an incredible coincidence given that both sides had been formed within a year of each other in the mid-1870s.

Although still in primary school, I recall the excitement when Essex made their breakthrough in the Benson & Hedges Cup Final against Surrey. Somerset followed a few months later with the John Player League and the Gillette Cup. Essex would culminate their campaign with the big one, the County Championship. The Fletcher-Gooch-Lever side would become one of the greatest dynasties in modern county cricket with nine further trophies in the 13 years that followed. In Botham-Richards-Garner, that Somerset side had three of the best players ever to feature in international cricket, let alone the county game. They would add three more one-day cups before imploding spectacularly in the mid-1980s.

Somerset remain one of only three first-class counties who have never won the County Championship. In fact there was an argument that no West Country side had won the trophy given Gloucestershire's three successes in the 1870s came in the unofficial era. Still Somerset's start this season had given them one of their best opportunities to take the title for the first time. The neutrals were firmly behind them.

Sam Cook's early departure had been a minor footnote from the win over Hampshire. However, the headlines surrounding his absence from this game were more worrying. A side strain was likely to keep him out for six weeks. Peter Siddle was drafted back in and Aaron Beard retained his place. The youngster may well have missed out had Cook been fit.

Essex won the toss and were 126/1 before capitulating to 216 all out in muggy conditions on a pitch offering considerable movement. Alastair Cook held the innings together with a patient 80 made over 186 balls in just over four hours. As in the eventual decider at Taunton, Cook's stoicism would be pivotal. That knock was the highest of this game, followed by his own 47 in the second innings. Somerset ended day one on 32/1 with Jamie Porter's enthusiastic celebration after snaring

Azhar Ali just before the close an indication of the game's importance.

I ummed and ahhed over going on day two or waiting till day three. However, the previous week, I had opted for the latter when faced with a similar question and missed the victory over Hampshire as Essex triumphed easily in five sessions. This time, I got it right. The first session of the second day would be pivotal not only in the game but the season. Porter and Siddle peppered the batsmen but could not make a breakthrough. Then the ball was tossed to Beard at the Hayes Close End. His first 15 balls would yield four wickets for just 11 runs as Somerset fell from 63/2 to 74/6.

The 22-year-old from Chelmsford has an athletic, fluid approach and slightly front-on delivery. The key characteristic was the angle of his run-up, which was around 30 degrees wide of an imaginary line between the two sets of stumps. It was reminiscent of the late, great Malcolm Marshall. Beard's third delivery swung away from Tim Groenewald, who was enticed to follow it and Tom Westley held on at third slip. James Hildreth top-edged a pull from the first ball of his next over and Nick Browne raced around from midwicket to hang on to a wonderful low catch at square leg. Three balls later, Tom Banton prodded at another outswinger and feathered an outside edge to Adam Wheater behind the stumps. At this point, Beard had bowled ten deliveries at a cost of five runs and picked up three crucial wickets. The second ball of his next over was overpitched and pushed through the covers for four by Stephen Davies. From the delivery that followed, the Somerset wicketkeeper mistimed a similar shot and dollied a catch to ten Doeschate at mid-off.

Beard played in the first game of the 2017 Championship season against Lancashire but had barely figured in the first team since then. He did not even bowl in the first innings of the game against Hampshire the previous week. However on Day One of this game he would finish with career-best figures of 5-1-23-4 to break the resistance of his side's main title rivals.

Rain forced the players off before lunch. After the resumption the seventh Somerset wicket would put on 40 before the final three fell for just 17. Jamie Porter ended the visitors' innings on 131 with a delivery that sent Jack Brooks' middle stump out of the ground without touching the other two. It gave him a return of 5-51.

Despite the gloomy conditions proving conducive to movement, the Essex top-order provided a firm foundation. At Chelmsford in 2019, 250 was a creditable first-innings score and a double-century seemed perfectly satisfactory in the second. In this game, Essex would reach 100/2 and 100/3 respectively but, in the latter, they shipped three wickets before bad light stopped play and were rolled over cheaply in the first hour of the following morning for 183. It all left Somerset chasing 269 over five sessions to win.

As I took my seat in front of the pavilion at the start of day three, it struck me as a quintessential British cricket day. There were sun hats and short sleeves despite some threatening grey clouds overhead. The hubbub in the pavilion was as much about the inconvenience of baggage searches at the gates and tutting at the tardy arrival of food as chatter about possibility of Essex ending Somerset's unbeaten run and hauling themselves on the shoulders of the league leaders. 'Twas ever thus.

Again, Essex set the tone with early wickets. Somerset were two down inside three overs. Tom Abell was caught and bowled by Porter from his second delivery; 13 balls later he had Ali caught at third slip. Harmer saw Banton caught by Browne from the final ball of his first over, then the counter-attacking Hildreth was tucked up by Siddle and snicked behind. A score of 64/4 at lunch was troubling for the visitors, whose approach had been positive verging on the cavalier. When they were reduced to 73/7 soon after the restart, I tweeted in my best David 'Bumble' Lloyd voice 'start the car'. Lewis Gregory swiped consecutive sixes off Harmer, but his innings of 40 in 34 balls was ended when Beard clattered his middle stump so hard that it chipped and had to be replaced. The youngster ended the game with match figures of 7-45 from 9.2 overs. Despite recording figures of 9-73, Jamie Porter had somehow been outshone again.

Still, Essex had now won all four home games this season, inflicted defeat on the leaders for the first time this season and had reduced the arrears in the County Championship table to 13 points.

The Grumbler

In June, I received an email on my Grumbler email address. It was from a production assistant at BBC Essex, the local radio station that covers the club. They had supplemented the excellent ball-by-ball coverage they began producing a decade or so ago with a Saturday afternoon cricket show, called *Around the Wicket*. It covered Essex CCC and the local leagues showing admirable enthusiasm in both areas. As a regular emailer to the ball-by-ball commentary team and vociferous Twitter user they wanted to talk to me as part of their regular Speak to the Fans slot. Little did they know that this request would force a change of direction for me.

I had always been pretty cautious about revealing my identity. The whole Grumbler persona had started when I had been asked to write a column for the club website. I thought a character would be better than straight think-pieces so I plumped for a name that was a gentle dig in the ribs at the stereotypical county member. I started a Twitter and Facebook account in the same name and kept them up even when my work with the county stopped.

Having previously held back from using social media in anything but sedate ways, I enjoyed the anonymity my handle gave me. I protected it. Part of the appeal of attending Essex games was the fact that I was doing my own thing, utterly and completely. Hiding your real identity was fine for the first decade or so but, in the last few years, social media had changed. Anonymity started to be considered sinister and dangerous so, for example, when I tried to restart my Facebook account after it fell into misuse, new regulations forced me to reveal more personal details than I wanted. I opted out.

The production assistant from the BBC also wanted to know my real name. Quite rightly, the corporation have strict guidelines on giving a voice to anyone who is unknown. I thought about declining the interview but then, I was hoping this manuscript would turn into a book and, although I could 'do a *Belle de Jour*' and go under a nom de plume, it seemed a little self-important. This is only county cricket after all. In the end, the deciding factor was accountability. My tone of voice is about guarding the spirit of the game. County cricket means something to myself and many, many other fans in England. Despite the bedrock of humanity at the heart of the game, I feel that a vocal minority of football fans could not care less about anything except their team's success. I had views about English cricket, strong yet open ones that were hopefully worthy of discussion. Anonymity had given me a little more confidence to be open and forthright. However, these days it was not enough.

I had been stringent about avoiding Twitter rows to the extent that I put it in my bio. Partly because it is often needless grandstanding that brought out the worst of both sides and most were simply a shouting exercise where debate was absent and heels were merely dug in further. But mostly because even when I felt I was right and articulated myself well, an argument would infiltrate my thoughts. It was likely to spoil that day and potentially the day after.

This was one reason football had begun to fall from its pre-eminent position in my sporting affections. Everything was disputed, everything was rancour and subject to argument. It was as if the fans wanted to replicate the moment where two footballers on opposite sides challenged for the ball near the byline.

It is clear to all that the ball goes out of play off one player but, instantly, eagerly and with utter conviction, both put up their hands. Everyone knows the decision but the losing player still harangues the officials. For many this is part of the game. For me, it is posturing that borders on the pathetic.

So I decided to go on the show and, for the first time in almost a decade, revealed a little of my identity. In part it was about getting over the terrible affliction of imposter syndrome that had held me back and caused so much unhappiness for so long. If you are reading this and my thoughts have been turned into a book then you will know that personal progress has been made.

The Hundred (and why many cricket fans fear it)

If The Hundred develops as the ECB proclaims then it will save cricket in the United Kingdom.

If The Hundred develops as many established supporters fear then it will mortally wound historic counties.

If The Hundred develops as my worst-case scenario then I will probably never watch another live, professional game again.

THIS MAY seem extreme given the motorway miles I covered watching Essex in 2019 and I truly doubt it will come to that. But the fact that it might merely hammers home the gravity of the situation. To coin a phrase from another divisive change playing out in the same year, this is not 'Project Fear'. It is the solemn concern of a supporter who always kept an eye on the price of a lifetime membership at Essex as I fully intended to spend a peaceful retirement on the benches in front of the pavilion. Those perennial back-of-a-cigarette-packet calculations discovering the optimum time of purchase stopped once the outline of The Hundred first emerged. Over the years, the County Championship has become my primary spectating format. A Twenty20 night was fun but inhospitable, 50-over games just dragged while Tests were too busy and expensive. So, if the worst came to the worst, what will I be left to watch in ten years' time?

In truth, sports never really die, they just cease to be shown widely on television and become tatty, Poundshop versions of their previous selves. Consider speedway, an Essex invention. It held a prominent profile in the 1970s and was among the UK's most popular sports. It can still be seen on satellite television but it has long been on life-support. Likewise, rugby league was resonant in my youth but has been slipping from view for decades.

Football has always been the UK's pre-eminent sport and, since the formation of the Premier League, has expanded to virtually obscure all others. But for many, it is now a grubby, gaudy circus; an international event on British shores where television contracts in China seem more important than sporting integrity or the welfare of ticket-buyers. There is growing boredom with the anger and infamy that first started spewing out of professional football when the cash started rolling in. Of course, 'the product' is better. The quality of play, the stadiums, the matchday experience and the coverage are all far superior to the pre-Premier League era. Meanwhile, the revenue the sport can generate has grown exponentially, even if its distribution is more skewed than ever.

In the same period, a number of county cricket clubs have come perilously close to extinction and, to steal a phrase from one CEO, others have been 'counting every loo roll'. Major sides like Lancashire needed non-cricket revenue such as concerts to keep their players in linseed oil while Durham were relegated, albeit controversially, after getting into financial difficulties. Most counties would struggle to stay afloat but for a sizeable annual sum from the ECB. This is often labelled as a 'handout' but it is actually payment for teams nurturing talent for the Test side, a key revenue stream for the sport. These funds, as much as £64m in 2015, keep the county game solvent and the governing body would argue this is only possible due to the highly controversial television deal that took Test cricket off terrestrial television after the 2005 Ashes series. The ECB have also used this money to improve everything from the England team to the grassroots of the game. It has funded facilities and many crucial schemes, including the excellent All-Stars Cricket that brings primary school children into local clubs for coaching. This long-winded economic background is important because we must avoid dichotomous thinking. This should not be a story of the heroic, saintly Davids battling against a big, bad, tradition-hating, money-grabbing Goliath. However, both sides are guilty of thinking in such stereotypes.

County cricket must change or it will wither away to insignificance. There is consensus on that. My argument is that the existing structure has shown enough green shoots of recovery to change via evolution. Those on the ECB's side seem to believe only revolution will do the job. The organisation had already sparked one global transformation within the sport at the turn of the millennium. Our rich industrial history has shown it is typical for such innovative thinking to come from these shores. Alas, it is also standard practice not to fully capitalise on these breakthroughs. Twenty20 cricket began in England and was an instant hit worldwide. India and Australia loved it so much they developed leagues much bigger and better than ours. It is a bare-faced fabrication to suggest that English county fans did not embrace this new venture. Yes, they may have treated it as a fun, knockabout version of the game in comparison to the more established forms but they turned up to watch. I was among 26,500 fans who attended the first-ever Twenty20 game at Lord's on 15 July, 2004. There was a sense of history around the occasion and I simply wanted to be there, even if Essex were not involved. Arriving late, the ground was so full that I had to heave myself up to the top of the Grand Stand where I saw Lance Klusener try to haul Middlesex to victory over Surrey with a few typically agricultural shots. A few years later, it was common for all the games at Chelmsford to sell out long before the first ball was bowled. The growth has continued since then. In 2019, almost 950,000 spectators attended games in the Vitality Blast, as it was now called. That represented a 15 per cent leap on the previous year and a rise of almost 50 per cent over the last five seasons. As you will find out later, Twenty20 Finals Day has long since usurped the one-day cup final as domestic cricket's showpiece. All this supports the notion that a two-division Twenty20 competition could have been developed with the top flight taking the prime August spot The Hundred would fill. This would have not only preserved but developed the appeal of the counties. A tournament such as this would not command the media rights fees of the new event but it would serve to strengthen the roots of the game, rather than destabilise them. Growth would be slower but much more robust.

There was criticism that, although Twenty20 was popular, counties had maximised revenue by targeting the Friday night, after-work crowd. This filled the stadiums and swelled the coffers as fans quaffed beer after beer but it was not attracting families and younger fans. There is mileage in this argument but you cannot blame cash-strapped counties for taking this route. As a governing body, the ECB's role is to balance-up revenue and the need to grow the game. The move to take England matches away from free-to-air television was all about the former, albeit with positive knock-on effects for the latter. Were not the counties doing the same thing, presumably for the same ends?

Hands were shaken on that deal well before England's success snatched the sporting agenda in the summer of 2005 but it was highly criticised at the time as a poor strategic move. Despite swelling cash reserves, few forward-thinking sporting organisations have looked back on exclusive satellite television deals as successful in the long term. Even the mighty Premier League have always maintained *Match of the Day* as a free-to-air highlights show to provide visibility for future generations. The United Kingdom considers itself a sporting nation but that does not mean we are willing to pay to watch game after game, even for football. Sky's audiences for key Premier League clashes are dwarfed by more minor FA Cup ties on the BBC, let alone major dates on the sporting calendar like Wimbledon and the Olympics, which statute deems so important to the general public that they are shown free-to-air. The ECB had to lobby their way off that restricted list to take Sky's shilling. It has been argued that the need to right the wrong of 2005 prompted the desperation to get cricket back on terrestrial television, especially the BBC. My point is that we mortgaged the farm and sold all the historic silverware within merely to heal this self-inflicted wound. We were not out of hope yet. Had a revamped Twenty20 been tried and failed then the new venture would have enjoyed much more support among rank and file supporters.

Returning to terrestrial television was strategically crucial for cricket, neither side can deny that. The 2019 Women's World Cup football tournament showed us how high-quality, free-to-air coverage can summon up hitherto unknown sporting passions in this country. It stole the public consciousness in the early summer even though the Cricket World Cup was being held simultaneously in England for the first time in 20 years. The BBC's blanket coverage meant the general public's water-cooler conversations centred on Phil Neville's Lionesses as much as Eoin Morgan's men. The only Cricket World Cup game that was shown free-to-air was the final, and even then only after much-reported wrangling behind the scenes. Naturally, Sky were reluctant to give up exclusive coverage of their biggest live asset that summer. It was the first cricket game shown on a terrestrial channel in 14 years but the viewing figures were heartening. Channel 4's broadcast peaked at 5.2 million, the combined figure with Sky's platforms was almost 9 million, and half of that number watched throughout. The Wimbledon Men's Final was being shown on the BBC simultaneously and the cricket had pushed the British Grand Prix to More4 but a staggering 15.4 million saw the final at some stage,

31 per cent of these watching the sport for the first time. This is not so surprising when you consider that young people voting in the General Election in December 2019 might have been only four years old when they lost sight of cricket on terrestrial TV. In that time the game had left our perception. It was absent from our television screens and, to a large extent, our school playing fields and then our village greens. However, the World Cup tournament saw 52,000 new domestic ticket-buyers purchasing 227,000 seats. After the final, research showed that '40 per cent of fans intended to follow cricket more in the next 12 months'. Couple that with the upwardly-mobile ticket sales for the Vitality Blast and surely there was enough foundation upon which to try and rebuild the game along its current lines. It is crucial to understand this background because, in my opinion, what would follow has demeaned the sport of cricket in the country of its birth.

The communication of The Hundred began with silence then built to a worrying, confusing cacophony of noise. A new tournament was originally announced back in March 2015 but at the start of 2019 journalists were still unable to tell fans about how it would play out. In February, one cricket correspondent wrote, 'only the skeleton of the playing conditions ... and the barest of operational frameworks ... had been agreed'. CEO Tom Harrison did not give a single interview on the matter in 2018 apart from one announcement. But, later on, the message that it was 'not for established cricket lovers' and other gaffes were mediated loud and clear. There was talk of alcohol-free stadiums and 'a laser-focus on families'. But these narratives only emerged after the previous lead angle, that 'the best will play the best', had been scuppered by the Indian cricket authority's reluctance to make their players available for the tournament. The names of the teams emerged without planned fanfare via website registration records and they used pop concert pictures which were not reflective of their much-trumpeted target demographics in promotional material. It was inevitable that The Hundred would downgrade one existing event and the 50-over Royal London Cup seemed to be the best option. However, this news seeped out just before the world's most important tournament was to begin in England. It was, of course, a 50-over competition. All these mistakes were far from hanging offences but, in terms of communications, they were obvious traps that the ECB failed to avoid.

A more serious crime against cricketing sensibilities came in the latter half of 2019 when the 'brand identities' of the new franchises were rolled out. The names, kits and badges jarred with traditional fans but that was probably the point and, in fairness, they were akin to those in the Big Bash and IPL. However, the marketing backstories to the teams were pure advertising hogwash. They were supposed to define the essence of the club but they just read like horoscopes. Apparently, the London Spirit had a 'unique ability to conjure something special' while the Welsh Fire were 'burning bright with intense passion and relentless energy'. How can anyone artificially inject meaning and purpose into a team that had never taken the field and whose players were yet to join? It was vague, vacuous and entirely tone-deaf to the sporting public in the United Kingdom. The same can be said for the sponsorship deal with KP, a manufacturer of crisps and other snacks. Australia's Big Bash tournament is supported by a fried chicken outlet – players are even interviewed in a giant KFC bucket. But the ECB had developed their new event with a clear intention to attract families back to the game so partnering with a firm manufacturing what the head of the NHS described as 'junk food' was always going to garner criticism when you are trying to attract the Mumsnet crowd.

A failure to reveal their supposedly-supportive research in a timely manner also worked against the ECB. At the start of the process, this information was continually referred to but not released. It was either cock-up or conspiracy but certainly, it was not clear, controlled communication. We were all well aware that many of the numbers surrounding the game were ominous. Participation had fallen eight per cent in the previous three years, and if you were counting regulars who played once a month it was down 20 per cent. The Hampshire League, once the world's biggest, had lost 40 clubs in that time while second and third XIs were becoming a rarity everywhere. ECB figures suggested that 10 million people professed to be rugby and cricket fans but 2 million actually paid to watch the former and only 1 million the latter. Only five per cent of young people between the ages of seven and 15 listed cricket in their top two sports. They argued that families wanted short, sharp entertainment and were not being served by the county game. Meanwhile, the gradual urbanisation of Britain meant the population identified more with cities than counties. This led to the notion that hosting games in city centres would garner greater attention and attendance.

This last point has always been the crux of the issue for me. The elevation of new, faceless city franchises over counties steeped in history, tradition and identity means I will always oppose The Hundred. The format was never the problem. Tests, one-dayers, Twenty20, The Hundred and even T10, it is all cricket to me. I'd support Essex if they played in any of these formats because they are part of my identity. They were my local team growing up, I first went to see them as a child with my father and then enjoyed a few raucous nights with club-mates. Our 1979 breakthrough victories in the County Championship and Benson & Hedges Cup came just before my tenth birthday. That is the time when fandom takes root. Since then, I have followed the county through thick and thin. As you will read later they brought me to tears on more than one occasion in 2019. I do not come from London, I come from Essex. They are different places. So why should I follow London Spirit, my nearest Hundred franchise? Somerset fans were even being asked to identify with Welsh Fire, a team from another country.

Sport is part of the entertainment business but it cannot be learnt via an MBA textbook because fans are not customers and customers are not fans. Surrey have a better ground than Essex and, for much of the past two decades, a more star-studded team. It just does not matter. They can have the best matchday experience, social media, marketing, commercial teams or whatever. They will not get a penny out of me, except when Essex play at The Oval. However, as I proved in late September 2019, I will spend a few hundred pounds to go down to Taunton to sit in the stands watching the rain fall as my side edge to the title and be thoroughly delighted to do so. I watch, I engage, I tweet, I try in vain to get my family interested. Not because of some well-written marketing copy, the colours of a kit or some indecipherable blurb outlining the identity of a team yet to play but simply because I care. Essex mean something to me. In recent years, more than I realised.

Modern sport is increasingly blind to this. It is full of career marketers, administrators and executives who discuss 'social good' and the 'love of the game' but, generally, are judged on revenue. That is why Harrison appears to have been nonplussed at some of the criticism and talked about The Hundred 'already being a success' a year before its first ball was scheduled to be bowled. He was merely trumpeting how much money the television deal had accrued. Yes, there was also a free-to-air television element but three-quarters of the games would still be on a satellite broadcaster. And anyway, being back on the BBC merely reversed the short-sighted decision that the ECB had previously made. At this point, any governing body will scream 'that was not us' or 'before my time'. However, to fans, you are the same people, representing the same organisation, wearing the same suit and displaying the same Teflon attitude. According to the 2018/19 ECB accounts, Harrison's pay rose by £114,301 to £719,175, reportedly because of the 'success of The Hundred' launch. This is a 19 per cent bump on a vast salary at a time when the general population were not long out of austerity measures and feeling lucky to get an extra two or three per cent in their annual pay packet. The argument will run that talent must be rewarded, especially when key targets are met. This is driving the future of the game. Yet, in truth, the future of the game is being driven to nets by their parents on a wet Wednesday afternoon in Braintree well before the clocks have gone forward. Cricket is held up by millions of volunteers giving up evenings and weekends to secure the next generation of cricket. These are the coaches, the club committee members, the umpires and especially the parents. They are the ones who are really 'inspiring generations' and they are doing it all for a higher purpose – meaning, identity and love of the game.

The Hundred will be deemed a success whatever it achieves. The rules of this particular game are rigged in its favour. In February 2019, the event production budget was reported to be £6m and each ground was spending £200,000 on marketing the month-long tournament. By way of contrast, Surrey normally spend £80,000 per season on the Blast, and they are the most moneyed county. The ECB are throwing the kitchen sink at this in financial terms and clearing the schedule to put their prized item in the middle of the shop window. As 2019 wore on, there were stories of escalating costs, which had eaten into the ECB's reserve fund. The overall cost of the new tournament was most often reported as £200m, a figure that could write off the long-term debts of all first-class and minor counties. Much later it would seep out that the tournament was not even set to make a profit in its first five years if the counties' payments were included in accounting calculations. After that news, you have to ask yourself 'what is the point?'

Yes, you could judge The Hundred's success on participation rates but it seemed strange to be expecting a young devotee of, say, Trent Rockets living in Leicester to strive to play for an ephemeral franchise who exist for one month a year when all the player pathways were leading them to Grace Road. The argument goes that

Leicestershire would receive much-needed money from The Hundred's existence but the process would starve them of attention and, more importantly, aspiration.

In order to provide the constitutional rubber stamp for the new tournament to take shape, each county would receive £1.3m per year. Debt-free Essex put up some resistance but most quickly fell into line, their parlous balance sheets giving them little option. 'I'm not sure even if they [ECB] offered us a million pounds a year that it would be enough,' one chief executive had told the *Telegraph* at the time of negotiations in 2015. It appeared that they signed on for a little more than that, but further calculations suggested the 'net gain' after other necessary expenditure would be between £500,000 and £700,000 for some counties. There had been devil in the detail.

In the past, the counties had been caricatured as bickering, one-eyed and stuck in the mud, possessing a pomposity that had blinded them to the parlous state of their game. But, from the outside at least, it seemed that the ECB were unable to maintain much of the control they desired; somewhat surprising given that the counties were always so dependent on a financial injection from the central body for their continued existence. Certainly the development of The Hundred always appeared combative more than collaborative. Despite having much to gain from the tournament, Surrey voted against some of the playing regulations and, as a result, it was reported that ECB chairman Colin Graves threatened to strip The Oval of hosting rights. Somerset's then chief executive was quoted as saying 'staying in the ECB's favour was vital for counties seeking to be awarded hosting rights for internationals and major matches'. Meanwhile, the Blast's ongoing success was ignored so Surrey and Lancashire took the unusual step of issuing a joint press release in July 2019 to promote their record-breaking figures.

Logically, there are too many counties in the UK. Many supporters will accept that. But the governing body has never had the appetite to grasp the nettle and allow natural wastage. They even used some of that Sky money to sustain them, others had their key executives funded. This important point should be understood whenever county fans talk about The Hundred. The ECB could have contracted the County Championship table in the last 30 years just by sitting on their hands and letting the market dictate. They would have been pilloried but, over the same period, numerous football clubs have suffered financial calamities that resulted in them dropping divisions or starting 'phoenix clubs'.

Of course, if desperate, there was always another possibility – intelligent, compassionate contraction. Two or three mergers in the Championship over the past 30 years may have eased some of the financial strain and encouraged other counties to take a more communal view. The Twenty20 sides could have stayed separate but, in the four-day game, only a relatively small audience would be affected by bringing together six teams to make three. Would it have been better to have Derbyshire/ Leicestershire and Worcestershire/Gloucestershire combining, retaining their names and county grounds than going out of business? Yes, county staffs would have been cut, festival cricket might be no more and there would be a whole host of history and tradition lost but some semblance of the previous 150 years would be retained.

I would hate to watch Essex/Northamptonshire play at Wantage Road but it would still have more meaning than going to see London Spirit at Lord's. The former would be partly composed of players that fans had seen come through over the years. Some would certainly be from Essex. This could not be implemented without blame, blood-letting and the loss of something special. It is managed decline, one of the hardest processes anyone can undertake and few sports organisations possess the necessary appetite. But instead, many fans fear we are seeing contraction by distraction.

The Hundred will consist of eight franchises in eight cities so the money and attention will be concentrated in counties based at those grounds. Therefore, at best, fans fear the remainder are in danger of withering into insignificance. At worst, like speedway, they will be left putting on unloved fixtures in inhospitable surroundings with little attention. Then, if required, the plug can be pulled with little or no fanfare. The only people who will care are old, and no one listens to them, right?

With an increased salary cap and collar plus new transfer compensation agreed, the ground rules have been laid for a football-style market that can be exploited by big clubs. For example, a tacit link between Surrey and the Oval franchise, or Nottinghamshire and the Trent Bridge outfit may become apparent in contract negotiations with players. A county trying to sign a red-ball player will be significantly more attractive if they can smooth the path to their sister franchise in The Hundred, which would double a player's annual salary in one big-hitting month.

Counties and their tenant franchises were always supposed to be separate. Their names danced around a shared history and location but studiously avoided creating a firm connection. Later it was suggested there were 'synergies', with, for example, Essex, Middlesex and Northamptonshire nominally feeding into the Lord's franchise. By the time the early marketing of the 2020 cricket season was pushed out we had seen this creep even further. Some of the major counties whose grounds hosted Hundred franchises effectively included entry to these games to members. It was indirect and you might have to apply but it was available. Others, like Essex, had arguably seen a reduction in the value of the membership package as, by the ECB's own admission, the 50-over competition was now downgraded. For me at least, free entry to the women's Hundred franchise at Chelmsford was no recompense. It also did not make up for the end of the much-respected Kia Women's Super League in 2019. The jury was even out over The Hundred's ability to foster English talent. The eight head coaches were all from overseas and Kolpak players would be heavily represented in the draft.

It has been argued that The Hundred will be a rising tide, bringing money and attention back into the game, therefore lifting everyone, including all the counties. Any profit would be ploughed straight back into the game. In the latter part of 2019, Harrison continued to talk with sincerity of his commitment to a structure of 18 counties. However, the actions of the ECB speak louder than these words and many fans were left unconvinced. The next suit can always say 'not us, that was them' if they need to be held to account. Trust has been eroded to the lowest point I can remember so now the game's governing body and a significant proportion of its die-hard fans appear at loggerheads. Traditional members feel their game has been unnecessarily mortgaged on attracting a new audience. Those who currently pay to watch are being sidelined at the expense of those who might. If the former voice their disapproval they are dismissed as old and irrelevant.

Essex fans have seen festival cricket gradually disappear over the past two decades – Ilford then Southend then Colchester have all gone. It was sad but understandable given the cost, the reduction in council support and the need to balance the books. The club have long preached the desire for sound financial management so these were congruent if uncomfortable decisions. They also pulled back from a mooted stadium development when the financial market crashed in 2008. They have shown the optimistic expediency of Mr Micawber in *David Copperfield*. Happiness lay in balancing the books and investing in home-grown talent. Joyously, they won the 2019 County Championship title with as many as nine academy products in their side. But what good has it done them? Other teams, who have mortgaged themselves almost into liquidation to fund stadium schemes, are now being rewarded with franchises that will secure their future. If my worst fears are proved correct, my fine county may become a ghost of its previous self.

This is not a black and white issue. Many county members are in denial over what domestic cricket can be in the 21st century. My online sobriquet as The Grumbler is a pointed dig as some of my number who never seem satisfied. But it is not just us. The overall management of the game has been myopic and short-termist over the last 30 years, swaying this way after one report and that way after another. Until recently, the England team had spent much of the previous few decades being outplayed yet, on those occasions when they are victorious, cricket still has the ability to take over the nation. It did so throughout a glorious summer in 2005 and again on two incredible afternoons in 2019. The sheer resilience of the game should tell the ECB its soul should not be sold. The denouement of the World Cup Final was complicated; few fans were sure of the rules of the super over before it began. But there was little chatter about a lack of clarity amidst the tsunami of excitement on social media after the game. Complexity, another issue cited in the research behind The Hundred, was not an issue. Meanwhile, if a millennial audience can only accept its entertainment in bite-size chunks then why are they watching three-and-a-half-hour superhero movies or playing video games for weekends at a time? And how did they grow up reading 750-page Harry Potter books? In the long term, substance always trumps style no matter what the generation. Despite its youthful focus, The Hundred has even played a poor hand on social media, launching a Twitter account late in the day, without the blue tick of authenticity and adopting a cheeky tone of voice that only fuelled more anger. There was also a noticeable absence of a gaming strategy, a major mistake given the family focus of the tournament. In the previous year, a free game like *Fortnite* had emerged to become a cultural phenomenon. A highly playable mobile and console title could have ignited an interest at the heart of the ECB's target demographic.

Numerous reports have suggested the broadcasters, especially the BBC, pushed against a county-based tournament and the ECB were more sanguine about using traditional teams. So 'Auntie' may be the real villain of the piece. However, previous decisions by cricket's governing body left the balance of power tilted against them. They were so desperate to make a change and so hemmed in by previous errors that they had little choice. Then there seemed to be a scramble to justify what they had signed. From this distance, it seems obvious there was no clear and consistent plan running through The Hundred. There were no details, they had little clear comeback to the criticism and did not respond convincingly to being questioned. This is what happens when you are making it up as you go along.

In October 2019, Graves and Harrison were questioned on The Hundred by a Parliamentary Select Committee. *The Guardian*'s Matthew Engel wrote: 'Almost nothing their three-man team said made any sense whatever.' He added: '[The MPs] were not well enough briefed to get behind the bland evasions to reach the nub of what every sane person in cricket knows (even those who dare not say it) – that the ECB's strategy of forcing their new hyped-up contest The Hundred on an unwilling game is completely incoherent, staggeringly expensive and potentially disastrous.'

As a result of all this dispute and disruption, many long-standing county cricket fans see the ECB as an enemy of the game, or at least 'their game'. They feel even that if The Hundred proves successful it is only because they have sacrificed so much to make it so. They know it is they who will pay the price for all those cheap tickets so they see spin and cynicism in every new pronouncement. This group will do their best to paint the tournament as a pyrrhic victory at best, ignoring the strategic success of getting the game back in UK living rooms and the enjoyment of oblivious youngsters and families watching the sport for the first time. It need not have come to this.

Having travelled the county circuit in 2019, I have seen enough passion, skill, honour and sportsmanship to justify my continuing faith in the game. This is sport on a higher plane – it deserves salvation. Indeed, it might be just what we need in these troubled times. However, over the same period, the development of The Hundred seems to have eaten away at its very soul. Bulldozering through a half-baked idea via a blunderbuss communications policy laced with a haughty invective may be working in politics these days but this is county cricket – lovely, glorious and chivalrous. We fans demand more.

No one can put a price on cricket's joy, a KPI on its personality or a CRM system on its role as England's beating heart.

However, at the same time, my journey also revealed that disunity and rancour have left county cricket far too fragile to be left in fumbling hands.

It deserved so much better than this.

Nottinghamshire v Essex
(and the lady in the way)

Trent Bridge, 2 July 2019

TRENT BRIDGE is renowned as the finest cricket-watching experience on the county circuit. I had visited a few times before Twenty20 Finals Day and, more notably, an Ashes Test in 1993 when Essex seamer Mark Ilott was making his debut. That England team contained four from the county – Gooch, the captain but batting down at five, Nasser Hussain at seven and spinner Peter Such being the others.

The recollections of Ilott roaring in were crystal clear as I travelled up to Trent Bridge but I only worked out where I was sitting that day because of the position of the pavilion. It was the same for Twenty20 Finals Day in 2006 when I had a short-lived role reporting for the club. I was perched in the press box for Leicestershire's victory over Essex in the first semi-final, then sat glumly on top of a double decker stand watching the Foxes defy the odds to beat Nottinghamshire. Both those vantage points were hard to locate because Trent Bridge has undergone a vast reconstruction in the past few decades. However, it has been achieved with considerable sympathy for the game.

I dropped my daughter at school then broke several speeding laws to reach the railway station early because, even if my train was on time, it would arrive 15 minutes after day three began. Then there was a 20-minute walk to the ground, albeit a pleasant one passing the grounds of Notts County and Nottingham Forest football clubs then crossing the river and finally passing the 'world famous' Trent Bridge Tavern.

Nick Browne had been lbw in the first over of the day, ending a career-best score of 163, his first century in two years. I heard the yelps of Ryan ten Doeschate falling the same way as I went through the gates. Essex were already leading by more than 100 after dismissing rock-bottom Nottinghamshire for 213 on day one and they would continue to pile on the agony. The tail-end batsmen added brisk 20s and 30s in support of Ravi Bopara's 135. That innings was only halted by a stunning catch by Stuart Broad, sliding in just before the boundary rope to grab the ball one-handed inches above the turf. Even veteran Bopara would say afterwards it was one of the best grabs he had seen. Before the catch, Broad had bowled 33 tiring overs. Who says England cricketers don't care about the county game?

Nottinghamshire had to score over 300 just to make Essex bat again. This grand old county were enduring a horror season but it did not seem to affect their members' affability. I wore an Essex cap at this game and, throughout the morning, found people staring, smiling and nodding, as if creating the opportunity for a chat. Being a natural loner and, some would argue, a typical Southerner, I did not engage. However, at lunchtime, I was cornered just in front of the pavilion. It was a perfunctory ten-minute tour through all the usual 'British' topics: the state of the teams, my travel up, the weather etc. Despite my reservations, I appreciated the gesture and lament that I rarely see Essex fans engaging in such openness. Then again, I am clearly part of the problem.

I sat in front of the old pavilion for the afternoon session as Bopara poured on the runs. It was a well-preserved building full of memorabilia. The players' changing rooms were found via a narrow, creaking staircase supported by a worryingly insufficient bannister. Before darting upstairs they would file through a corridor barely wide enough for more than one person and lined with black and white pictures of committee members in uniform wooden frames. On the opposite wall there was a large board showing the club presidents throughout history and a couple of County Championship-winning pennants hung from the ceiling. There was a bar at the back and, in front, a large room was reserved for those who were content to watch the game through glass. Although the old-fashioned feel of the pavilion was out of keeping with this otherwise modern arena, I appreciated the small museum at the rear, the luscious cream cakes that emerged for sale at tea and the white coats worn by the stewards who stood each side of the entrance. These little touches are not just important, they are 'the difference'. The surroundings at Trent Bridge show more care than the majority of the sports venues I have ever visited. Even the fonts and graphics used on the signage suggested a certain cricketing class while the stewards wanted to swap pleasantries, even when you merely asked for information. Most English of all was the sign calling for minimal movement behind the bowler's arm. The promised punishment would not be banishment from the ground or fine but embarrassment. And we all know that is a most powerful crowd-control tool in Britain.

Midway through the afternoon, as I watched from in front of the pavilion, there was a tapping noise from the rear. A lady of pensionable age emerged in an overcoat and a Nottinghamshire sun hat. She was visually impaired and seemed a little hesitant in using her white stick. She bumped down the steps outside the pavilion and, with the help of the steward, found her way to a nearby seat. Blind fans at sporting events are not rare. There are sections for such supporters at football grounds where they can listen to specialised commentary while experiencing the audio aspects of the atmosphere like everyone else. I expected this lady to pop on headphones and take in the excellent online audio provided by BBC local radio. But she did not. She just sat and listened to the sounds of the game.

For me, it begged the question: what was she getting out of being there, given that she was only consuming the cricket audibly? To her, was not the game just a series of murmurs, knocks, claps and general hubbub? Then I recalled my mother's comment when I took my parents to Southgate for an Essex game a decade or so earlier. She'd been a merry cricket widow for decades in her younger days, often reminiscing about the friendships among their Sunday team; the men playing, the women watching, chatting and making the teas. These were the 1950s and, in my mind's eye it was all picnics, dotted handkerchiefs, Lambretta mopeds and, by modern standards, overt sexism. Still my mother talked lovingly of those days and, though barely a fan, was content enough to watch the occasional day of cricket on retirement if it was a family event. On this occasion at Southgate, having barely looked up from her knitting throughout the day's play, she ventured: 'I always enjoy going to the cricket, I just like the atmosphere.'

Southgate was one of the smaller outgrounds on the circuit, lined with hedges and gloriously nestled in the shadow of a church spire. Give the ground a sepia tint and it seemed but a short step from a forgotten England of the Women's Institute, choirs, Sunday roasts and jumble sales in which my mother revelled. So, I assumed, the visually impaired lady at Trent Bridge that day 'just liked the atmosphere' and the sense of camaraderie.

At tea, the lady decided to move into the aisle just at the moment the teams were trotting up the steps. One of the quaint traditions of cricket is that players leave the pitch by walking between the seats where members are normally seated. This can mean that, just moments after a batsman is dismissed, he is within earshot of his fiercest critics. I have seen players react to comments as they pass through and part of me is surprised at the infrequency of these events. Certainly few other sports could keep this sort of tradition in the modern world.

The players who came off at tea did not have muttering county members with which to contend but the shape of an elderly lady unexpectedly blocking part of the aisle and seemingly oblivious to their presence. But then both cricket and cricketers are nice. After the odd quizzical look, they all skipped around her and darted into the pavilion for tea. Despite only having a 15-minute break, a couple of them popped back out to speak to youngsters who had come up for the day.

Having worked in football for the entirety of my career, I felt increasingly disdainful at the lack of humanity that had taken over the game. In the last 20 years many tunnels and walkways to the pitch had been designed to temporarily extend outwards when players were using them in order to protect them from abuse, bile and general nastiness. Even in smaller grounds stewarding had become an almost impossible job because of fans' angry expectations. The increase in prices brought forth the argument of: 'I have paid my money so I can ....' Of course this meant that they were increasingly held back from connecting from the players and the club, the very opposite of what they demanded and expected. The humanity has been extracted from a very human experience. So while football would accuse cricket of not moving with the times, cricket could snap back: 'Look where it's got you – rich but angry and unhappy.'

As you get older, all this hangs heavy on your shoulders. The concept of the angry young man and calmer veteran is not just part of sport but music and politics. Bands often talk about 'the difficult second album' and success stifling creativity. Meanwhile, recent elections have proved once again that the population generally become more conservative, with a big and small c, as they grow older. You mellow in middle age partly because your priorities change, partly because you have seen the same patterns play out before and partly because you are too darn tired to fight with the ferocity you did. The cult of youth is stronger than ever. Despite the ultimate democracy afforded us by the internet, our media is seemingly dominated by a tiny percentage of the young, fit and permatanned, even though they may have nothing positive to contribute to society. Unfortunately, Essex is the spiritual home of this phenomenon in the UK. When I attend Championship games, the spectators are much older and quieter than the *TOWIE*-watching generation. But do not go away thinking these are all sad old men, though many are sullen and the vast majority are male. This is a pocket of peace and understanding in a world that is increasingly hard to pin down. Everyone will age and change, even those Instagram influencers flogging charcoal toothpaste.

I sneaked out just before the close with Essex utterly in control. My train was leaving at 6.30pm. On the platform was Graeme Swann, the former Nottinghamshire and England spinner, who was on his way up to Durham to commentate on England's World Cup game against New Zealand the following day. Despite his abundant ability and successful career, he will always be remembered for retiring in the middle of the 2013/14 Ashes tour after England went 3-0 down. This must be a pressure-cooker environment, one which requires deep reserves of mental fortitude. Still, for those of us without the talent or capacity for graft to ever get in that position, it is hard to understand.

On the train home I felt heartened. The game was secure and, indeed, Essex would complete victory by an innings and 123 runs, 40 minutes after lunch the following day. It was their first away victory of the campaign and their fifth in the last six. Somerset hammered Hampshire at Taunton in the same round of fixtures, taking eight wickets in the first session of the final day when most had assumed the visitors would have to be prised out on a docile pitch. They had clearly returned to form. However, Essex had the greater momentum and they were back at Fortress Chelmsford for the next two games before the hiatus for the Vitality Blast.

Essex v Yorkshire
(and absence of ice-cream)

Chelmsford, 8 July 2019

FOR A time in post-war America, it was thought that ice-cream might be the cause of polio. Researchers into this debilitating, life-threatening disease had noticed that new cases spiked during the summer months in close relation to the consumption of the freezing cold confectionery. They argued that increased sugar intake was the driving force. This famous mistake is one of the prime examples used to identify the difference between correlation and causation. Just because A and B happened at the same time does not mean that A led to B or, for that matter, B led to A. Only valuable research can clearly define a connection.

Deep down, County Championship fans know their type of cricket is not the future of the game. Despite the finesse and purity of four-day fixtures, the main economic justification for its continued existence is to provide a pipeline of players to the England team. This is fundamental. Every single England international player has come through the county system or its forebears.

However, that does not mean the Championship is irrelevant and there is an ad hoc movement among fans to promote its continuing popularity. A number, including myself, started ridiculing the idea that no one attends these games by tweeting pictures of well-stocked stands with captions trumpeting: 'Proof: No one turns up to county games.'

I did this on day two of this game with Yorkshire. The members' car park was full and taking no more new entrants 45 minutes before play was set to start on a bright Monday morning. By my estimation there were 1,500 supporters in the ground when play began. On the Sunday, fans were tweeting that the ice-cream van had run out by mid-afternoon. Like those polio researchers 75 years ago, it would be dangerous to infer too much from facts like these as Essex is a well-supported county who were enjoying another title run and, even then, the crowd is drawn from older sections of society.

Of course, there is an argument that the audience is latent or remote. I would say 'sleeping' but that implies a few of the septuagenarians were dozing off after a pint or two in front of the pavilion. The visitors for this game, Yorkshire, had 59,000 supporters during their 2015 title season, a jump of 39 per cent on the previous year. The final game winner-take-all affairs in 2016 and 2019 also brought big crowds to four-day games. But the revenue would have been superseded by one packed-out, full-bellied Twenty20 game.

Along with Surrey and Lancashire, the Tykes are one of the few teams to always bring a visible amount of travelling fans to Chelmsford for Championship games. Only 36 points straddled the top three and so Yorkshire still had one foot in the title race after completing victory over champions Surrey at Scarborough with minutes to spare in the previous set of games. A hearty victory in this fixture would have brought them parity with Essex. A year earlier, Yorkshire had been rolled over for 50 in the first innings at Chelmsford, only to recover and win the game. But, even without Ravi Bopara and Sam Cook, Essex would have their noses in front throughout this encounter.

Yorkshire captain Steve Patterson surprisingly elected to bat after winning the toss. Perhaps the thought of chasing a total in the fourth innings against Simon Harmer nudged them into a counter-intuitive approach. However, it was worth Patterson gambling as, according to Cricinfo, he had won each of the last 11 tosses he had contested. The odds on that were 2,048-1.

Jamie Porter had a loud appeal for lbw against Adam Lyth from the first ball and would eventually have the opener caught at slip for 5. Then Peter Siddle plucked out the leg stump of Gary Ballance to leave the visitors 37/2. However, the Essex bowling would mix their usual penetration with a host of 'four-balls'. Yorkshire played positively and reaped the benefit. Harry Brook top-scored with 46 and wickets five to seven contributed 108 of their 208 all out. It seemed meagre but few visiting sides would muster any batting bonus points at all at Chelmsford in 2019. However, Harmer's 5-76 was anything but unusual.

The Essex batsmen knew their pitch all too well by now. Their eventual score of 328 was probably worth more than the 519/9 at Trent Bridge the previous week. Nick Browne and Bopara had been the bedrock at Nottingham while Cook had been the key early in the season at

Chelmsford. This time, Tom Westley (81) would lay the foundations then Ryan ten Doeschate's unbeaten 70 was the glue in the middle order alongside crucial contributions from Siddle and Aaron Beard. The eighth- and ninth-wicket partnerships added 106, a huge difference in the complexion of the match. At the end of the second day Yorkshire were 38/3 after Wheater produced a superb low catch to dismiss Ballance and Tom Kohler-Cadmore swiped horribly across to line to be caught in front by Harmer. It would get worse in the morning when they slumped to 58/5, still 70 short of making Essex bat again. They recovered to 129/8 but it seemed a matter of time. Then Kesh Maharaj changed tactics, thumping 16 from the next four balls he faced. The South African spinner hit five sixes and seven fours in an innings of 85 from 71 deliveries. It took a low skidding delivery from Siddle to remove him with the score on 193. The last-wicket pair lifted Yorkshire to 211. Essex would use less than 22 overs to chase down the target of 92 and complete an eight-wicket victory.

For an hour or so, Essex were one point clear of Somerset at the top of the table. However, Nottinghamshire would lose eight wickets after tea on day three to subside at Taunton after earlier belying their lowly position and threatening a surprise victory. In Dom Bess and Jack Leach, Somerset had a breadth of spinning options comparable to Essex on their own ground. They had taken 14 Nottinghamshire wickets while Craig Overton had picked up the other five. Chris Nash had retired hurt. The cricketing press were now defining the season by these two sides and fans of both must have been starting to compare scores.

However, if anything, the matches against Yorkshire and Essex were much closer. On both occasions, a tail-end partnership would be the difference. Siddle and Cook's stand meant ten Doeschate's men had avoided defeat at Headingley while, at Chelmsford, Beard joined the captain in a key cameo that, in the light of Maharaj's effective aggression, set up the victory. This was important to remember as Somerset were travelling to Yorkshire in the next round of games.

While the Championship was bubbling up nicely, the World Cup had found its finalists. New Zealand beat India in a rain-affected game and England dominated Australia in the last four this week. Eoin Morgan's men had endured a patchy run to the final but they seemed to be hitting form at the right time.

'We are sometimes homesick for the places we have never known'

Essex CCC might have gone out of business around 1966 and 1967. Their overdraft was so large the club had to instigate 'ruthless economies' and began a series of fund-raising measures, even redeeming Green Shield stamps to help the cause. This was a period of disharmony. The club distanced itself from its own Supporters' Association for a period after the latter lost faith, stopped its funding and decreed that specific financial requests would be considered by its committee before action is taken. The staff was slashed to just 13, one of the casualities being talented all-rounder Barry Knight, who had lost the battle with Brian Taylor to succeed Trevor Bailey as captain. He cut ties with the county and moved to Leicestershire.

Essex finished 16th in 1966, in part thanks to a dip in Bailey's form as the threadbare squad meant he was forced to play on with a leg strain. The club played festival cricket at Leyton, Westcliff, Colchester, Clacton, Ilford, Brentwood, Southend and Romford that year but lost money on six of the eight venues. They wanted to buy the freehold of their ground at Chelmsford but they simply did not have the money.

Bailey operated as not only captain but secretary until the start of 1966 when the club appointed Major C.A. Brown in the administrative role. The new recruit had to roll up his sleeves. As *Sunday Mirror* columnist Ted Dexter wrote: 'He was quite likely to be seen putting on the covers, marshalling the cars, doing the books and cajoling the team in the space of one hour.'

Bailey is rightly regarded as a titan of Essex CCC. Not just for 28,641 runs and 2,082 wickets in first-class cricket between 1946 and 1967 but for keeping this struggling outfit going in its darkest days. However, according to the *Essex CCC Official History*, he believed his major contribution came late in 1965 at a dinner to celebrate Worcestershire's victory in the County Championship. He met up with some Warwickshire acquaintances and mentioned Essex were struggling to finance the purchase of the Chelmsford ground. By the time the night was over, the Warwickshire CCC Supporters' Association had offered an interest-free loan of £15,000, a staggering £238,000 in 2020 money. Who knows where Essex would have been but for this act of largesse?

Along with this donation, Essex were held together by the will of a few key individuals and pocket change of their public. The bucket was regularly passed around the crowd at this time. They had to innovate too, so, in May 1966, Essex became the first club to host professional cricket on a Sunday when they entertained Somerset at Ilford. It was not legal to charge admission at the time but around 6,000 fans attended and a welcome £500 was raised through scorecards, stand seats and collections.

While the departure of Knight was lamented, 'Tonker' Taylor proved to be the right type of captain for the situation. As David Lemmon puts it: 'He insisted on standards of dress, blazer and tie, and fitness.' The threadbare Essex squad was put through a demanding pre-season regime and turned into one of the best fielding outfits in the country. This was particularly beneficial to their one-day game. Having been hopeless in its early days, Essex were third in the inaugural John Player Special League in 1969, fourth in 1970 and finished their final game on top of the table in 1971. However, Worcestershire beat Warwickshire inside 18 overs at Dudley the following week to win the title on a faster run-rate. Essex had been denied their first major honour by 0.003 of a run.

The paucity of the Essex squad in the early era of Taylor's captaincy meant youngsters had to play. The experience gained by the likes of Keith Fletcher, John Lever, Ray East, Stuart Turner and David Acfield in that period surely provided a platform for the sustained era of success that followed a few years after 'Tonker' stood down in 1973.

There are always lessons like these in history if you are prepared to take a step back. Sometimes we call them the good old days just because we cannot remember them so well. Who knows, perhaps the furore over The Hundred may come to be seen as just a storm in a tea interval? While many have grave concerns, others have meditated on the issue and declared 'this too shall pass'. Indeed, just as 1966 led to 1979 for Essex, county cricket could emerge much stronger for this disruption. Of course, there is always the possibility that the tournament will provide all the money and attention the ECB promise. Given the gamble involved, let us hope they are right. But even before a ball was bowled, it bound together a large number of well-meaning county supporters for a common purpose and, seemingly, against a common foe. All manner of benefits may emerge from that in the years to come.

Essex v Warwickshire (and missing the World Cup Final)

Chelmsford, 14–15 July 2019

AS YOU may have worked out by now, a sense of displacement had followed me for a few years. Over this weekend, I would feel all over the place. For a start, this game should not have been held at Chelmsford. World Cup engagements at Edgbaston had meant the original game was switched to New Road, the home of neighbours Worcestershire, at the start of the season. I had mentally ringed the game in red as this ground has a reputation as the most picturesque on the county circuit. On the banks of the River Severn with an old-fashioned pavilion and the cathedral in full view, many opine about its virtues in almost Arlottian terms. However, New Road is also susceptible to flooding. The two most widely seen non-playing pictures in any cricket season are a couple of fans huddling from the cold in an otherwise empty stand on the opening day of the season and Worcestershire's ground underwater. The former is an annoying newspaper staple, an easy jibe against the county game by editors filling space. One year, a radio commentator pointedly asked a publication on social media why they had deliberately printed a picture of a stand that was roped off that day. Worcestershire's problems were all too real, however, and their groundstaff deserve immense praise for creating the conditions for cricket despite this perennial problem. When the floods hit New Road this year the simple solution was to flip the fixtures.

The switch meant Essex had another home game, very useful in maintaining momentum given that they were boasting a 100 per cent record at Chelmsford and the visitors had been hit harder by call-ups to the England Lions squad. Matt Quinn replaced Jamie Porter in the Essex side. Warwickshire were missing Sam Hain and the in-form Dominic Sibley, whose heavy run-scoring in 2019 would eventually lead to selection for the England Test team. Former international Ian Bell was not yet fit so the visitors called up 18-year-old debutant Dan Mousley, who had only been given a professional contract a month before, and Michael Burgess, an on-loan wicketkeeper who would play as a batsman. There was another major absentee for Essex. Long-serving scorer Tony Choat would be the official recorder of the World Cup Final, which was taking place on day two of this match. I arrived on the opening morning and cheekily posted a picture of a healthy crowd with the caption 'Yep, no one turns up to County Championship games on a Saturday'. It was a little mischievous as the notion that attendances naturally increase on the weekends seemed somewhat unproven on this day. A former team-mate of mine always hated seeing young people in the crowd at Essex games on Saturdays and Sundays when they could have been playing the game.

Still, there were regular Monday to Friday workers to consider. Indeed, the 2019 fixtures had originally appeared without weekend cricket only for an outcry to see them altered. Significantly, this round of games saw Somerset visit Yorkshire, a side who had nearly beaten Essex and, on paper, one of their toughest remaining tests.

It was an overcast day so Warwickshire chose not to contest the toss and insert Essex. Again, the top order would pass 100 for the loss of only two wickets. This time Essex reached 157 before Alastair Cook was the third batsman to be dismissed. The mood music around him was still a little sombre. As ever, the opener had not listened, instead grinding away innings after innings at his own tempo. He had been steady if unspectacular, the right approach for a Chelmsford strip on which 250 was a creditable score. He hit 84 in the first innings of this game and 83 in the second. It would be the third time Cook had been top scorer in both innings of a home match. It was the second time he scored more than 50 in both innings and took his season's average to 47.50. At the start of the 2020 campaign, at the age of 35, he would finish top of the team's pre-season fitness tests. According to rumour, he has never been beaten on a 'bleep test', the ultimate examination of aerobic capacity. Since he first broke into the Essex side, it had become a look-at-me world. Reality stars, especially those from Essex, were famous for nothing and constantly hijacked our attention by fair means or foul. As I had become more insecure in my career, a sliver of such behaviour had become normal for me. It was not arrogance but I noticed a greater propensity for self-justification and rolling out credentials in working situations. Perhaps this was part of the self-promotion you require as a consultant but it made me entirely uncomfortable. The old adage that 'confidence is quiet, insecurity is loud' never rang more true. From the outside, Cook has always seemed entirely comfortable in his own skin, not shy or reserved, just unflustered by the pressurised world in which he chose to reside, whether he was playing cricket or knee-deep in 'work' on his farm. At the end of the season, I tweeted the local City Council to request the team be given the Freedom of Chelmsford. This was not really a joke; however, I may have weakened my argument by adding that this would allow Cook to drive his sheep over the famous Army and Navy roundabout in the centre.

His 116-run partnership with Dan Lawrence was the backbone of the Essex first innings. The latter was out seven runs after his more illustrious colleague and the lower order collapsed either side of tea with Will Rhodes, a first-change bowler and former Essex loanee, taking 5-17. However, the last two wickets contributed 48 runs with Peter Siddle providing enough fortitude for a batting point then Aaron Beard hitting 29 in a last-wicket stand of 34, as Essex gained respectability to reach 245.

Five overs from the end of play, just after Beard had carved the ball to point and picked up three, the players briefly left the field when an air ambulance hovered over the outfield and threatened to land in order to assist a sick spectator. I had left a couple of minutes earlier but heard the noise as I walked to the car park in a field just off Meteor Way. As I approached my car, I noticed a very different disturbance; a couple were having open-air sex in the long grass. To quote the long-lost *News of the World*, 'I made my excuses and left'.

Day two of this match also coincided with England and New Zealand contesting the World Cup Final. But I was neither at Chelmsford nor Lord's. In fact I was in a field with a dubious internet connection trying to follow both games at once. I grant you this was an odd decision, but not as strange as Championship cricket being scheduled on the same day as the biggest one-day game in England for over 20 years with the hosts always among the favourites to qualify.

An inexperienced Warwickshire side were reduced to 33/4 and only a last-wicket stand of 27 hauled them up to 161 all out, a deficit of 84. Peter Siddle took the plaudits with 5-33, including two in four balls. Like Cook, this experienced campaigner had been displaying quiet quality throughout the campaign without truly hitting the headlines. The Australians had been blitzed by England in the World Cup semi-final three days earlier and now their focus was on the upcoming Ashes series. Siddle would eventually make the squad and his performance today would have been a nudge.

When stumps were drawn on day two, Essex were 73/1, a healthy advantage of 157. At that point, Somerset were following on at Yorkshire and, most urgently of all, England required 78 from 63 deliveries at Lord's to become world champions. They would get 77 but completed a joyful and historic victory in the super over. Day three started with cricket front-page news for once.

I was jumping for joy when Jos Buttler collected Jason Roy's throw and stretched to his left to whip off the bails before Martin Guptill got home. But, as often, with such triumphs my exaltations were to an empty living room. I had only seen the first 20 overs of the New Zealand innings and the last ten of the England reply. In the intervening time I had taken my daughter to a football tournament. My cricket spectating and my wife's hectic work schedule meant it would have been morally reprehensible to do anything else. So I tracked the progress on Cricinfo on the way up, used a month's supply of data to stream patches of play on the sidelines between football games and dodged the attentions of numerous speed cameras to hurry home. I even had to make a sizeable detour to drop off one of my daughter's team-mates, whose parents I bloody well hope were saving a life somewhere.

However, I made a pact with myself long ago that I would try to prioritise key personal moments over sporting ones. More or less, I have kept to that. Not that I have had an easy ride with either in my 40s, and what determines 'key' anyway? Still, I think my percentage of school plays and sports days attended stacks up reasonably well against most working fathers. Albeit I spent many of the performances trying to ignore the phone buzzing in my pocket. In truth, the tournament had dragged for the latter half of the groups and, as previously discussed, was in danger of being overshadowed by England's female footballers. After decades of seeing our cricket teams' soft underbellies cruelly exposed, it was heartening to see them tough-out a victory under intense pressure. Ben Stokes was simply brilliant. Though, for me, New Zealand's sportsmanship and humility in defeat was just as impressive. How would our fans and media have handled that deflected boundary with three balls left and the subsequent controversy about the additional run England were handed in error? One of the most shared videos of social media afterwards showed Kiwi captain Kane

Williamson on the pitch being told he had won the Player of the Tournament. He listened intently, looked back at the media executive and exclaimed: 'Me?' Reportedly the New Zealand team simply cannot sledge convincingly – it is just not 'them' so they stopped. This has all combined to create a positive brand around their team. This time, the good guys were wearing black caps. Having lost the last two World Cup finals, it would be beneficial for the image of the sport for Williamson's team to land a top prize. Cricket could do with their own Jack Nicklaus or Roger Federer. Match-fixing had blighted the reputation of the professional game and somehow the idea that you had to be loud-mouthed and aggressive permeated the game. In the past decade, stump microphones picked up all sorts of revealing off-the-cuff remarks. The stock of Joe Root rose sharply when he rebuked an opponent for using a homophobic slur, likewise Buttler blotted his reputation with unprovoked, foul-mouthed abuse of Vernon Philander during the tour of South Africa in early 2020. Cricket should copy the NFL's lead and impose heavy sanctions for bad on-pitch behaviour. What is the point of all the work in the community and with schools if your heroes cannot act as role models? This should be considered part of an elite athlete's discipline along with training, resting, eating and focusing.

The morning after the final, about the time the England squad were assembling at The Oval for a World Cup celebration, Cook was punching a four through extra cover to bring up another 50 at Chelmsford. In truth, Essex might have already had enough to beat Warwickshire given Harmer's ability to run through a side in the second innings on his home patch. However, ten Doeschate would declare only when the lead reached 400. Brookes had Rishi Patel caught from the first ball of the first over after lunch then castled the captain from the last. Ten Doeschate turned to look at the pitch as he walked off. Presumably, he had mixed emotions given signs of lateral movement was in the interest of Essex given their sizeable lead.

Lawrence accelerated the scoring, first with Adam Wheater and then Simon Harmer. The latter even strode down the pitch and smacked Rhodes for a straight six. Both batsmen were eventually out slashing across the line straight after tea without adding to the score. There were grumbles from fans about a late, defensive declaration from the captain. This sort of myopia is infuriating. Surely you had to back a leader who had led the club to promotion and then a fairy-tale title. If this game ended in victory it would be the 24th out of 37 games since returning to Division One and might put the team back on top of the table. Apart from the 1979–92 team this was the greatest time to be an Essex supporter in almost 150 years.

Warwickshire were 67/1 at the end of day three and put up admirable resistance the following morning. It was only the second time an Essex home game had reached the last day in 2019 and I was back in the Tom Pearce Stand for a sunny Tuesday. Siddle made the breakthrough then c Cook b Harmer accounted for two wickets in two balls. The visitors' batsmen counter-attacked with Burgess and Brookes pilfering a host of sixes. The size of the Essex advantage meant it did not matter. Harmer took 6-75, taking him to 64 Championship scalps in 2019 as Essex won by 187 runs.

An hour or so earlier, Kesh Maharaj had dismissed Craig Overton at Headingley to complete Yorkshire's victory over Somerset by an innings and 73 runs. On a turning wicket, the Taunton team had been deprived of Jack Leach due to England Lions duty. But it was hardly an excuse for the hammering which brought just one bonus point. They had also lost heavily at Chelmsford a week or so earlier.

As a result, Essex went into the break for the Vitality Blast on top of the County Championship table for the first time in 2019.

Middlesex v Essex, 18 July 2019

My son was slumped at the dining room table, staring downward and shaking his head. I had been trying to sell the occasion. 'It's Middlesex v Essex … start of the Twenty20. It's at Lord's … the home of cricket … a full house … 25,000 … loads of big hitting … loads of razzmatazz … much more exciting than the 50-over stuff at Chelmsford.' Tickets had been hard to procure but he just did not want to go.

That day, the esteemed sports journalist Martin Samuel had written a prescient piece with the headline: 'Don't blame Sky if your child is not into cricket, look closer to home.'

'Just about every sportsperson of any standing thanks a parent or teacher for their sacrifice,' he wrote. 'And some haven't the time and some haven't the inclination. Far easier then to blame Sky or the ECB and fondly imagine that putting the Ashes on the BBC would somehow spirit your child into the Under-11s at the local cricket club if you were still in bed when the match started at nine o'clock each Sunday morning.'

I can plead not guilty on that particular count. Dad's Taxis was a thriving business in our house, taking my children to training sessions in football and swimming. The latter even involved getting up at 5.30am twice a week. I had also coached my son's football team for two seasons. The atmosphere for our Sunday morning games was sometimes regrettable thanks to a small percentage of the adults involved and the attitude they allowed their children to project. However, it was fun to coach once more and I found that the afternoon before our weekly sessions would be diverted towards researching drills. Yet, there was a major crime on my cricketing rap-sheet. Despite being a long-term club participant, qualified coach and vocal advocate, I had given up playing the game. Though I had never seen my father play I was aware of his exploits and it was telling that he kept yellowing newspaper clippings of them in a drawer until his dying day. Had my children biffed a ball around on the boundary while I huffed and puffed in the middle then just maybe they would have taken up the game. I feel guilty about that. At some point, every father realises that you can give wonderfully sage advice and turn up to every event in good time, but your child's ability to copy is greater than their ability to listen. That is why when you become a Daddy, it is Daddy who has to grow up. It was by far the hardest part of parenthood for me.

However, I remain an active campaigner for cricket of all codes. A few weeks earlier, an American pal offered me a ticket to Australia v New Zealand at Lord's in the World Cup group stages so I spent a happy day dodging

the roasting sun and explaining to him the mechanics of
the game. A Dutch friend would make his debut with the
Twenty20 ticket my son did not want. Lord's on a sunlit
summer's evening is simply stunning. From the precision
of the field to the architecture of the pavilion via those
sweeping three-tiered stands, everything is just perfectly
so. We watched Essex compile a seemingly competitive
164/6 thanks largely to ten Doeschate's unbeaten 74.
The visitors were in the game until AB de Villiers came
to the crease in the sixth over with Middlesex on 39/2.
The South African pillaged six sixes and five fours in
an unbeaten 88 which averaged more than two runs per
ball. Even my Dutch friend understood Essex had been
hammered.

The following night, Cameron Delport would outdo
his compatriot with 14 sixes and seven fours in an explosive
129 from 49 balls as Surrey were similarly demolished
at Chelmsford. It was the first win for new Twenty20
captain Simon Harmer. However, rain and regrettable
performances would blight their early progress in the
South Group.

Kent v Essex
(and the hollow half-century)

Canterbury, 19 August 2019

IT STARTED hammering down just as I arrived. This was not the light summer rain that leads to an in-and-out kind of cricket day, it was stair rods crashing down from a slate-grey sky. The game was 30 minutes from lunch on day two and Essex had been trying to end some late-order resistance after Mohammad Amir and Sam Cook had scythed through the leading Kent batsmen on the previous afternoon. The latter was playing his first game in six weeks after recovering from a side strain. The former was playing the last red-ball game of his career. A few weeks earlier he had announced his retirement from Test cricket with Pakistan. From now on he would be a white-ball specialist. It is a decision that made economic sense. His earning capacity was considerably higher in the short-form game and, unshackled from Test matches, he had the freedom to hop from tournament to tournament following the sun. Besides, bowling short bursts of four overs per game would prolong his career. Many a paceman lost speed, confidence and years of earning potential by pounding the treadmill of Test match bowling.

Despite all that, it was a shame in a sporting sense. Amir was one of those lithe left-armers whose skiddy delivery could castle a batsman and bring crowds to their feet. He had been brought over for the Twenty20 campaign and, according to the press release, agreed to play this solitary Championship game before his retirement had been made public. He was filling a vacancy left by Peter Siddle, whose early season form had led to an Ashes call-up.

Amir had played a crucial cameo in the 2017 title, most notably in the two-day destruction of Yorkshire at Scarborough. At the end of the Kent innings today he had taken 18 wickets in his Essex career at a cost of 13 runs each. They were stats reflecting his quality and, in a sense, the gulf that exists between the elite players and the county trundlers.

With all due respect, Darren Stevens is the personification of the latter. He had spent 22 years on the county circuit, the last 15 of those at Kent. What was left of his hair was grey and any pace that remained was dwindling, but this all-rounder had produced a host of match-turning performances against Essex. His game was now based on guile and experience, maximising his potential and so becoming one of those players who had seemingly been around forever.

This was his 300th county game, it was Amir's last. Two vastly different players drawing from vastly different talent pools with vastly different motivations. Despite typically fine form this season, Stevens had not been offered a new contract by Kent and was actively looking for a county. Alas, I arrived too late to see the slim Pakistani bowl to the stout Englishman. That would have helped this story. Amir did not even get him out, Stevens was lbw to Cook. But then, this was not a storybook kind of day.

It was my 50th birthday, a milestone that I had tried to ignore for a few years. Completing each decade inevitably leads to reflection – there is much in the section to follow. The only difference with this one was that I was now unfailingly, unrelentingly and without qualification, old. At 40, you can fool yourself that you are doing everything you were at 30. The following decade had been draining physically and, by now, some joints had started to creak. If you add narrowing career possibilities, death or illness of parents, general bewilderment at modern life and you reach 49, which is renowned to be the most miserable year of all. Therefore, on the upside, I had put that particular bastard to bed. Secondly, my dotage, of which I intended to spend the majority at Chelmsford, would be much jollier.

It was entirely in keeping that my birthday would be spent cowering at the back of the Frank Woolley Stand as the rain swept over the St Lawrence Ground. Firstly, I like nothing about such celebrations, probably because of the attention, the need to be happy or the thought of advancing years. I had tried to ignore them most of the time but, in truth, the inevitable self-reflection and circumspection actually makes me sad. Not unhappy, not miserable, just wistfully melancholic. That, and the chance of seeing Essex increase their lead in the Championship, meant Canterbury was the perfect place for me to notch my personal half-century.

I'd been once before, to see Kenya v England in the 1999 World Cup. The famous lime tree just inside the boundary rope was already diseased by then and the resulting weakening saw it succumb to high winds six years later. A replacement sapling was not big enough to take a hit from a cricket ball so it was planted outside the playing area. Thus ended one of the greatest tales in county cricket. The Lime Tree Café on the site was the most noticeable echo today.

Otherwise, the ground was typical – old stands named after heroes, newer executive boxes and a line of apartments down one side. A supermarket at one entrance was a nod to necessity but, thankfully, the famous grass bank on the opposite side was intact. It was from there that a jazz band trotted out some old favourites during the intervals. It made for a pleasant ambience as 'Mac the Knife' etc. fused with the general hubbub and floated across the ground. This game was part of the 168th Canterbury Week, the oldest cricket festival in the world. This one saw a couple of Twenty20 games sandwiching this four-day game. The first one-dayer had been called off without a ball being bowled. Rain had demolished much of the Twenty20 Blast schedule and presumably put a huge dent in county coffers. The Twenty20 to come at Canterbury was also expected to be hit by rain but this game was supposed to survive virtually unscathed. It did not.

A couple of severe downpours had curtailed yesterday's play and, against all predictions, the same occurred today. I would see about 50 runs and two wickets spread across both sides' first innings. At 5.21pm, play was called off for the day. My round trip was over three hours, about three times the amount of cricket I had actually seen. Some might say that is a pretty poor birthday but my expectations of these occasions are pretty low. Anyway, these days are part and parcel of cricket, especially the county version.

Typically the following day would be a bone-dry, sun-kissed cracker packed with drama. Essex had walked off at a soggy 32/1 the previous night and, one presumed, only a score of 350 plus would give them enough time to force the victory required to extend their lead at the top of the table. Somerset were struggling at Edgbaston and seemed likely to gain a draw at best so opportunity knocked for Essex at Canterbury.

The visitors reached 40/1 before Alastair Cook was dismissed. They would lose five wickets for 27 runs in the following 15 overs and started to stare defeat squarely in the face. Adam Wheater and Amir hauled them to 114 all out but it was still the lowest Essex total of the season and a full 112 in arrears. However, one of the bowling spells of the season would turn the game.

Kent were dismissed for 40 in 18 overs and one ball with Sam Cook taking a stunning 7-23. It was the fourth-lowest total in the history of the Garden of England county and their worst in 149 years. Kent were 7/3 after Cook picked up a wicket from the second delivery of the innings and then Amir grabbed two inside three balls. The first of those came courtesy of a magnificent low catch by Simon Harmer at second slip. Then Cook dismissed Zak Crawley and Ollie Robinson to make it 9/5. When the same bowler produced a penetrating inswinger to catch Stevens in front to leave Kent 19/7, Essex fans could start to believe in the possibility of victory. History had shown we could never do that until the old warhorse is out. Porter knocked over Matt Milnes' off-stump to end the carnage. No Kent batsman had reached double figures.

That still left 153 to chase, a sizeable score in the context of the game. Again Alastair Cook's dismissal caused a slump, from 51/1 to 52/4. When Ryan ten Doeschate fell to make it 84/6, Essex still needed 69 with four wickets remaining. I started running half-hourly Twitter polls as to who would win – Kent were nearly always favourites. Hardly Jon Snow-like rigour but it told a tale. However, Wheater and Harmer took Essex within 12 runs of victory and Amir's final batting stroke of a red ball was a flick to the on side that completed a memorable victory on a day in which 26 wickets had fallen, 12 of which were lbw. For once, Simon Harmer, the country's leading wicket-taker and future *Wisden* Player of the Year, did not even turn his arm.

I had to watch this unfold on Kent's YouTube channel, which I synced with online commentary. This feed of two static sight-screen cameras and the pleasant old-style patter from a combined team of BBC Essex and BBC Kent held my attention all day, completely ruining the work I had planned to undertake. Contrast that to the mini-villages that camp themselves in Premier League grounds to run 30-strong camera teams fronted by super slick presenters who talk us through every angle. This is brilliantly produced, state-of-the-art sports coverage and yet often struggles to hold my attention in comparison to a low-scoring four-day game when my team are fighting for victory. Speaking of comparisons between our national sport and football (see what I did there), let's talk about Wheater's dismissal in the first innings.

Just three balls before the Essex wicketkeeper was out, he had seen Amir caught by Heino Kuhn to end a 43-run partnership that had taken the Essex first-innings score from historically poor to merely horrible. Yet the Canterbury pitch was dangerous when the ball was hard but demure when it softened. As a consequence, quick and heavy scoring felt possible in the lower order. Wheater is an accomplished batsman whose modest average belies his ability. Short in stature and undemonstrative at the wicket, he relentlessly attacks almost irrespective of the situation. Coming in at No 7, he was accustomed to marshalling the tail. In 2012, I had seen him smash 98 from 111 deliveries to put Essex one shot from victory against Hampshire in the County Championship. Having put on 40 for the final wicket, Wheater was caught on the boundary going for the big hit that would have completed both the victory and his century.

He had moved to Hampshire and back since then, eventually winning the race to succeed James Foster as Essex wicketkeeper. Sam Cook and Jamie Porter occupied the last two Essex batting places at Canterbury so Wheater knew he had enough nous alongside him to be optimistic of extending their score by 30 or 40 runs. This could be a critical difference in such a low-scoring game. But when wicketkeeper Robinson claimed a catch from Harry Podmore's delivery and umpire Paul Baldwin stood motionless, Wheater did what cricketers all over the land are supposed to do. He turned on his heels and walked. Podmore, Robinson and the slip cordon had appealed loudly but their arms were dropping to their sides and they were looking quizzically at the umpire when Wheater started leaving the crease. The official may well have been waiting for the batsman to decide but there was no nod or indication. Most cricketers would have put the onus on the umpire, hoping for the benefit of the doubt.

This was a vital wicket at a vital moment in a vital match. Given the state of the two games, you even felt that the County Championship title was on the line. With just three games left, a significant advantage would be accrued if Essex won and Somerset did not, or vice versa. Yet, without ceremony, Wheater gave himself out. It has been suggested that Colin Cowdrey, English batting legend, Kent's most famous cricketing son and a famous 'walker', sometimes did so in lesser games in order to maintain his reputation with umpires when he needed to stay put. Who knows if that is true? The ethics of walking in modern-day cricket are a battleground between its romantic past and hard-headed present. However, Adam Gilchrist's global standing certainly went up when he walked against Sri Lanka in the 2003 World Cup semi-final and Stuart Broad's went down when he did not against Australia in 2013.

Having tweeted furiously about the game all day, my victory post was centred not only on the fact Wheater's honourable walk could have cost Essex the game, but he had actually gone on to win it for the visitors. It was shared to such an extent that, despite my following of only 500, over 28,000 people saw that tweet. While the Essex victory had been full of cricket's peculiar and often painful undulating drama, this match redoubled my belief that the game still retains its lofty position upon sport's true roll of honour and that fans are invested in preserving it.

The hollow half-century

It is no coincidence that this book was written in my 50th year. The more I read around the topic, it had become apparent that most studies suggest the trajectory of our happiness is not as we might think. Contentment does not shine brightly in our youth and then inevitably taper off into a maudlin grey fog penetrated only by tea, *Homes Under the Hammer* and short visits by disinterested but dutiful relatives.

Actually, life satisfaction was U-shaped with the bottom of the curve occurring around our half-century. Yes, our younger years were considered to be generally happy. These were carefree times where every avenue was lined with potential. Your body functioned perfectly, you looked as good as you ever would and your mind was not hauling around the baggage of envy and anger from battles lost. One never seems to remember it that way though. Many people recall their teens and twenties as insecure times when you know you are supposed to be in the prime of your life. But you feel you are not coming anywhere close.

Insecurities and lack of life experience can amplify mistakes and mishaps to the point where they can be emotionally debilitating. Social media has multiplied the problem. All of us can compare their inner monologue with the superficial outer narrative spun by the 'beautiful ones' on our devices. These days we should worry about the 16-year-old shop assistant in Harlow who can compare themselves, daily and directly, with a trust fund kid from California. Never mind that the former might be kind and generous while the latter has enough time, money and narcissism to take 200 pictures a day before posting the one that stands out. If, God forbid, that Essex boy or girl has some obvious imperfection like obesity, protruding teeth or spots then it will take thick skin and tremendous willpower to join this game of status comparison. All this still applies in middle age, only now you are comparing hairlines and waistlines, houses and spouses.

Your half-century is the age at which you are holding on to the remnants of a younger self while simultaneously being dragged down by the weight of an older one. The cliché 'life begins at 40' is wearily rolled out in conversations about middle age. Certainly it is an important milestone. But it was more relevant back in the 70s when couples were having children in their mid-20s, and the offspring were leaving school by the time the big 4-O came around. The world is different now. When I reached 50, my youngest child was not even halfway through her school education and, though I was among the older parents at the gate each morning, I was hardly ancient by comparison.

That said, it was an age at which grandparents were becoming too old to help out. If you are 50, your mum and dad could be 80 or beyond, which takes them into a period generally associated with ill health and decline. It is always painful to realise those you love are deteriorating. You muddle through day-to-day life barely perceiving a change until an old photograph or casual remark will bring the truth crashing down. By 50, you start to realise how far you crossed the line from career to carer, even if you only do it remotely. Couple that burden with children going through a torture of insecurity in their teenage years and you have a recipe for stress. Then, of course, there is your own status anxiety. This is the multiplier for many. To a major extent, we all judge each other on our jobs. If asked the question 'What do you do?' you will reply with the name of your occupation. The very language defines our identity, as does the answer, 'I am a ...' The problem was I did not have much of a reply anymore.

Supposedly your 60s solves this through the welcome death of ambition and the comfort of acceptance. This is one reason your happiness starts to take an upward curve. As American philosopher Henry James observed: 'How pleasant the day we give up striving to be young – or slender.' However, I still had an angry drive and supposedly two decades of working life left in me, but could not find a fulfilling employment solution. I had the luxury of choice, of course. My wife was doing so well in her job that it only made sense to switch responsibilities if I returned at a high level. However, no one seemed interested in putting me up there again.

Speaking of privilege, let's be clear. I am a white male and those two facts alone afford me a significant advantage over most people in the UK. We are inching closer to gender equality and, to its credit, cricket has been at the forefront of female sport in the UK ever since the indomitable Rachael Heyhoe Flint was elbowing her way on to *A Question of Sport* in the 1970s. The scales are only tilting a touch but even then some men have started howling in protest. That said, the so-called 'crisis of masculinity' is real as it is based on their expectations and self-perception, especially in the job market. My fear is that this will only get worse by the time the millennial generation reach middle age and, as author Simon Sinek explained, realise that constant confirmation that they were special may have left them unprepared for what is to come.

Let's hope they cope better than many of the braggadocio bankers my school spewed out in the 1980s. Back then, the cocky, wedge-haired, leather-jacketed kid flicking paper pellets at the rear of the class and stubbornly refusing to engage his street-smart brain tended to end up 'in the City'. He worked hard, made 'loadsamoney' and enjoyed debauched Friday nights 'uptown' drinking lager top. However, many of these men re-emerged 20 years later, cleared-out, worn-out and wondering what the hell happened.

The term 'midlife crisis' was first used by psychoanalyst Elliot Jacques in 1965. Since then, it has become a cliché. From *10* to *City Slickers*, *American Beauty* to *Breaking Bad*, Hollywood has ploughed this trough, telling stories of a spectacular reaction by men of a certain age when they feel life has started to shut them down. Cricket has a hand in this. Have you noticed how many ex-players have had hair transplants? Surely the sport over-indexes in this area.

In early life, we all tend to think of ourselves as the leading actor in our story with everyone else among the supporting cast or even just extras in the background. We all feel like the leaders of our own personal rock band, the sensitive Paul or the edgy, acerbic John writing the soundtrack of our own lives. For some of us, reaching 50 brings the stark realisation that you have been a pale imitation of Ringo all along. Stuck at the back, overshadowed by others and struggling to keep up at times. The irony is that even though the drummer has never been considered the driving force behind the Beatles and had the least solo success of the Fab Four, the man born Richard Starkey has always appeared admirably comfortable in his own skin in the latter part of his life. His most enduring Beatles contribution remains the perfectly imperfect vocals on 'With a Little Help From My Friends', the second track on *Sgt. Pepper's Lonely Hearts Club Band*. These days, the 79-year-old closes his shows with this much-loved track then walks off stage leaving the audience with the words 'peace and love is the only way'. Such is the sanguine wisdom of the life that awaits us all beyond 50.

* * *

Less than a week after the game at Kent, cricket would take over the nation once more when Ben Stokes and Jack Leach shared the ultimate last-wicket stand in the third Test at Headingley to keep the Ashes alive. Their 76 runs in 62 balls represented nine more than the entire England team had scored in their first innings. However, 362/9 represented the highest chase in their history. Stokes had been a World Cup-winning hero six weeks earlier, this time he hit a staggering 135 not out. At times he was so tired he just bent over and stared at the floor when Leach was facing. The Somerset spinner was resolute and hit the most famous 1 not out in England history, using the break in overs to clean his glasses. As *Wisden*'s report quipped, 'One batsman could not watch, the other could barely see.' Leach should have been run out but Nathan Lyon fumbled, Stokes should have been lbw but Australian captain Tim Paine had tossed away a crucial review. When the Durham all-rounder punched the winning boundary his roar was heard all over the country. It was not only an England victory but a very English one, too. This nation adores a match-winner, especially when they come back in such spectacular fashion. However, it showers a special type of attention on an unlikely contribution from an unheralded underdog. England would draw the series so Australian retained the urn. But the summer had shown that cricket, in its existing form with all its existing flaws, could still cut through.

Warwickshire v Essex
(and the soulless meeting)

Edgbaston, 12 September 2019

IN THE movies, there is often a moment just before the finale when all seems lost. The bad guys have employed their dastardly powers to wrest control or the lovers are parted through some sort of confusion or misunderstanding. These plot twists are employed to create tension and make the happy-ever-after that bit more joyous.

An empty Edgbaston on a midweek morning in September felt about as far from Hollywood as one could get, but still, in their third-last Championship game, it appeared Essex had blown their opportunity.

By the time I arrived in Birmingham at the start of day three, there was no chance of a seventh straight win. By his own admission, ten Doeschate had misread the pitch and erred in inviting the home side to bat. After two days of toil, Warwickshire had amassed 517 and the visitors had lost Alastair Cook at the start of their reply the previous evening.

Essex held a wafer-thin two-point lead over Somerset at the start of this round of matches. It seemed set to go down to the last game but, like Boat Race-coxes, both sides were jockeying for a crucial advantage that would dictate their tactics for the final sprint to the finish line.

On day one at Taunton, the home side had lost two wickets on 199 to fall one run short of a batting point. However, they then skittled Yorkshire for 109 and, by now, were compiling a match-winning total in their second innings. They would be leading the table once more at the end of these games – the question was by how many points.

This game was supposed to have been played at Essex but, to recall that convoluted tale, Warwickshire's substitute ground at New Road, Worcester had been flooded so they flipped the fixtures. Away members were let in free by way of recompense.

As my congested morning drive had demonstrated, Edgbaston is close to the centre of Birmingham, and like most sporting organisations in major cities, had developed a conferencing business in the last couple of decades. Understandably the fixture change was not deemed disruptive enough to cancel bookings.

Therefore, as I walked towards the dark blue, 1960s-style entrance, I was greeted with the cream of the UK's window business on a fag break after the early sessions of the Glazing Summit, whose website promised to 'tackle the biggest industry issues, including barriers to growth, sustainability, regulations, mergers and acquisitions, the skills shortage, smart tech and the future of the industry'.

There might have been more people at the conference than the game given that the official attendance was less than 300 on day two and it seemed little better 24 hours later. Warwickshire had endured a tough campaign and would have been odds-on to be relegated in the usual two-up, two-down season. However, Nottinghamshire were worse and they would be confirmed as the solitary relegated team at the end of this round of fixtures. Still, for a big city club, that was a poor crowd, and remember, I have seen enough of Essex in the depths of Division Two. Somerset, albeit challenging at the other end of the table, were boasting around 2,000 on the same day.

I had not been to Edgbaston for well over a decade. It was the second day of the 1997 Ashes series when, having dismissed Australia for 118, Nasser Hussain and Graham Thorpe would put on 288 for the fifth wicket. The Essex batsman finished on 207, the highest score of his career, as he punished Shane Warne and set up a rare England win. To be honest the occasion had melted in the ether of my memory banks apart from the vision of a drunken spectator, dressed as a Vegas-style Elvis, running up and down in front of my stand and shooting a finger gun at an Aussie fielder on the boundary. In fairness, he saw the joke and fired back at 'The King'.

Edgbaston was suitably impressive, drawing comparisons to The Oval before the roof on the OCS Stand was opened in 2014. Still, opposite the tall, impressive pavilion, were some rather tired-looking executive boxes and a small, old-fashioned and unsatisfactory scoreboard. For one of the major UK grounds, it felt a little lopsided. However, there were nice touches, such as the floodlights in the shape of an 'e', the Bear awnings on the gates and the memorable moments displayed in the concourses.

The club opened suites at the top of the main stand to give patrons a glorious view of the game with the Birmingham skyline looming in the background. The weather was mixed and the starkness of the grey skies over the tall buildings in the cityscape only served to bring out the greenness of the pitch in the sunlight directly below me. There is something about the cocoon of county cricket that can make you feel you are operating within an altered reality. I perched myself on one of the high tables and hauled out my laptop. As I settled down, one local leaned over, looked at my Essex cap and, in broad Brummie, said: 'Nailed-on draw eh?' I agreed though neither of us questioned the sanity of sitting there all day to watch this assured result play out. Such is the unspoken madness of County Championship followers.

The pitch was benign but Cook was out and, if Essex followed on, they would have to withstand the wiles of former New Zealand Test spinner Jeetan Patel for a sustained period. His opposite number, Simon Harmer, had bowled one ball short of 60 overs in the Warwickshire innings. Peter Siddle was now with the Australian Test team and Amir's one-game deal was over so Essex had no overseas player. They used eight different bowlers as they struggled to contain Matthew Lamb, who compiled 173 in a seven-hour innings. The visitors thought they had dismissed him on 110 when Harmer threw down the stumps from the slip cordon after Alastair Cook had spilt a catch. The visitors appealed and the umpire declared him out only to rescind the decision as Lamb had only left his crease because he thought the former England captain had held on. It was reported both that the officials made this call using a new rule and that Essex forced the umpire to retract the dismissal by withdrawing their appeal. I hope the latter is true.

The visitors' reply was held together by Tom Westley's 141. They were 299/8 facing the final ball of the 110th over, needing a single from the next delivery to secure another batting bonus point. However, Beard could only find a fielder in the covers. It could have been important. The visitors subsided to 324 all out and were forced to follow on. Westley had been an England player in 2017 before being discarded after five Tests and was the subject of a formal approach by Kent midway through this summer. From the sidelines, it seemed as if he had lost something after his international experience. Who knows, perhaps he went through his own redefinition in 2018 and early 2019? Certainly, in the latter part of this season, his return to form would provide a crucial backbone for the batting in both trophy runs. His first-innings knock lasted over six hours and ended 15 balls before the last man was out. Westley was back in the middle after five balls of the follow-on after Nick Browne was caught. He was out three-and-a-half hours later just three runs short of his second century in the game. The captains shook hands on a draw four balls after that. Essex had held on but Somerset's straightforward victory gave them an eight-point advantage with two games remaining.

At the start of my day at Edgbaston, I had used the lift to get to the top floor at the Pavilion End where I enjoyed those wonderful views. Pinned to the wall, just above the buttons was a list of meetings for that day. Executive box four on level three was set to host 'The Hundred: Marcoms and Ticketing Update'. As the premier cricket venue in England's second city, Edgbaston was always going to get a franchise. The ground was already visibly preparing for the Vitality Blast Finals Day in nine days' time. I had secured my ticket a few days earlier. That would be an all-singing, all-dancing, all-drinking party. The comparison between that wild night and today would have been apparent to anyone looking out of the executive box window in that meeting. It was a soulless scene in both senses and a tangible argument for urgent change in county cricket.

It is crucial that fans be a part of this process. Part of the furore surrounding the launch of The Hundred always concerned the lack of consultation with all parties, not least the supporters. But fans need to present their views with diligence and dignity. It is not just a case of being anti-everything, especially that which impacts their own county's interests. Any entertainment industry must respect its patrons but, on the flipside, pertinent points are easily swept aside if there is no true signal amidst the noise.

Thankfully a couple of clear, consolidated voices have emerged in the last few years, both with women at the helm. In 2017, the Cricket Supporters' Association was co-founded by Beckie Fairlie-Clarke with the intention to 'listen, campaign and make a difference'. She said: 'Free from commercial pressure, the Cricket Supporters' Association is uniquely placed to be a unifying force across England and Wales, bringing together all disparate groups and speaking on their behalf with an independent and trusted voice.' In early 2020, a fanzine called *County Cricket Matters* would start up under the editorship of Annie Chave.

There appears to be a movement forming; let us hope it can bring positive pressure to bear. The Hundred may have been the catalyst but the entire nature of following a county team has altered in the past decade. With considerable interest among a latent and remote audience, it was always vital that cricket connected with those away from the ground once technology allowed. Changes in media distribution created the opportunity. A decade or so ago the ECB produced a state-of-the-art smartphone application, with a scoreboard straight from the scorers' laptop among other innovative features. Around the same time, their website started to publish daily highlights packages from County Championship games. It was single-shot footage from the performance analysis cameras on each sightscreen so you merely saw play from behind the bowler's arm. When there was a catch in the deep you saw the shot, the bowler and infield fielders stare vacantly at the sky in anticipation before reacting in delight. But this was so much more than any fan had received before and, crucially, it was not just clip after clip. It was an editorialised report of four or five minutes with an intelligent script and voice-over. Years before that, BBC local radio had started to provide ball-by-ball commentary of every domestic game for each county. In 2018, some counties synced live feeds from those sightscreen cameras with this audio providing a basic yet absorbing television-style coverage online.

All this has deepened my interest in Essex CCC and, as the Kent game had proved, sometimes put a dent in my productivity. In earlier decades, the desire to keep up with the team's score saw me churning impatiently through

Ceefax pages, waiting through the endless preamble of expensive Clubcall phone lines or clicking furiously as Cricinfo refreshed. These days I spend my summer with one ear glued to the audio service and consult the live feed when time allows. The knowledge and camaraderie between commentary teams are part of the fabric of county cricket these days. The same men, plus a few women, talk about the same teams for every game from April to September, each year. This cannot be well-paid – most will be motivated through a love for the sport and desire to be involved in some way.

The ECB and BBC, two organisations who have drawn much criticism for their roles in the inception of The Hundred and its subsequent threat to county cricket, have enabled this new avenue to thrive. Developing this sort of content over such a long period and with such consistency sucks up money, time and focus. There was no obvious, direct, measurable financial return on this investment. Presumably, it was just another strategy to grow the game. Without question, it has worked. Somerset CCC recorded 2.1 million views of their redeveloped live stream during the 2019 season, a 400 per cent increase on the previous campaign. Over 80 per cent of the viewers were from the UK but there were 4,500 visitors from Japan, 2,300 from Thailand, 1,700 from Ukraine and 1,200 from Finland. Also, Somerset's video clips were viewed 49 million times on social media, a 1,000 per cent uplift from 2018, and its website set another record of 6.1 million page views.

Not all of these encouraging statistics are down to the ECB but it has to take a fair share of the credit. While some of the ire of county supporters is justified, it does fans a disservice to paint them as without virtue. It also allows those in charge to dismiss any dissenting voices as detached and ignorant of the rigours of modern sport. This merely increases division and creates a disharmony with which a sport like county cricket can ill-afford to be shackled.

Essex v Surrey (and the death of a thousand 'nos')

Chelmsford, 16–17 September 2019

ESSEX CAME into the penultimate round of County Championship fixtures eight points behind Somerset. By the time they actually started their match with Surrey at Chelmsford, that lead had stretched to ten.

Bad light prevented play beginning in Essex until 2.15pm on Day One and, in total, 50 overs would be lost. During that time, Somerset had reduced Hampshire to 135/7 at the Ageas Bowl and picked up a couple of bowling points. However, an eighth-wicket stand of 92 between Liam Dawson (103) and Keith Barker (40) eventually lifted the hosts to 196 all out and Somerset were 30/2 at the close. At the same point at Chelmsford, having won the toss and chosen to bat, Surrey were 137/4 with Ben Foakes looking in punishing form.

With the table so tight it was always likely to be a winner-takes-all game at Taunton the following week. The importance of this set of matches was to determine who would take the title in the event of a draw, something that seemed highly likely as the long-range forecast for Somerset was so poor that, at one point, a total washout was being predicted on all four days.

After the first three sessions of this game, it seemed Somerset's title to lose once more. However, like the weather, the fortunes of Essex would become much brighter and clearer on day two. Under near cloudless skies, Surrey lost six wickets for 37 runs as the hosts wrapped up their innings inside an hour. Sam Cook and Jamie Porter shared all ten wickets equally, a feat that allowed the latter to pass 50 Championship wickets for the fifth successive season. Each one was greeted by loud cheers from almost 3,000 spectators. News of each Somerset scalp at Hampshire rippled around the ground like a verbal Mexican Wave. However, on the instructions of the coaching staff, the PA did not relay the score during play on some days. And there was much to report because, while Cook and Porter were ripping through reigning champions Surrey, Kyle Abbott was putting on a one-man show on the south coast. By 11am, Somerset's three key batsmen, Tom Abell, Tom Banton and James Hildreth had been dismissed inside ten balls for the addition of seven runs to leave them 45/5. Abbott had got two of them and would get another seven in the innings.

Not that this was a stress-free day. The members' car park was so full I struggled to find a space an hour before the first ball, prized seats in front of the pavilion were already being guarded by deserted sweaters and, at 11.30am, the lady in front of me in the queue for food was told by a harassed-looking bar person that they had sold out. Such are the perils of watching cricket at Chelmsford on sun-kissed September mornings when Essex are closing in on the title.

I walked around the perimeter and posted pictures of spectators enjoying the cricket in the stands. The club would enjoy crowds of almost 7,500 over the three days of this game to complete a Championship aggregate of 34,813. A Yorkshire supporter posted a similar shot of a packed Headingley for their match with Kent which had little competitive interest. Their aggregate for seven home games in 2019 was 54,861.

The night before, Manchester United Women had played Arsenal in front of 2,500 at Leigh FC. It was televised live on satellite TV and there were numerous reports in the national media. This was an exceptional crowd. The women's major teams had been getting 1,500 the previous season with the average in the top division just tipping four figures. However, we had just enjoyed a fantastic Women's World Cup, pushed vigorously by the BBC on free-to-air TV. It had even snatched attention from the cricket World Cup until England's late resurgence. There was hope it would be the springboard for an improved Women's Super League this season. Having covered the sport a decade ago when it was not so trendy, this would be most welcome. Still, despite this concerted effort, the size of crowds in women's domestic football in the UK is small, so was the income, certainly no bigger than county cricket. Yet its perception was very different. Perhaps cricket's older audience made it less valuable for advertisers and that impacts the interest of television but, if we are honest, the bigger factor is that society values pensioners as less important than nearly every other age group.

Alastair Cook was lbw to a sharply-angled delivery from Jordan Clark midway through the afternoon to leave Essex struggling on 53/3. Surrey had little to play for but coach Michael di Venuto had given his side a public dressing down after the previous week's abject performance at Hampshire. Ryan ten Doeschate's heroics at The Oval on the final day of last season had spoilt their chances of repeating the unbeaten campaign of Essex in 2017. That was a fractious and unforgettable afternoon, the kind that sticks in the mind and elicits revenge. This could be the coldest of servings.

Elsewhere, the Somerset tail was wagging furiously. The pitch at the Ageas Bowl seemed to be a minefield when the ball was hard and new but a millpond when it was old and soft. Dom Bess and Roelof van der Merwe helped them recover from 65/8 to 142 all out. That was still 54 behind after both first innings and Abbott's figures of 18.4-9-40-9 illustrated his dominance but the visitors were still afloat. When they reduced Hampshire to 10/3 and 103/8 later in the afternoon they must have been buoyant.

Meanwhile, Essex were rebuilding. Dan Lawrence and ten Doeschate put on 173 for the fifth in 40.2 overs in the latter two sessions of the day. The Englishman reignited last season's talk of an England call-up with powerful driving before he was dismissed for 147 just before the close of play on day two. At that point, Essex were leading Surrey by 128 with four wickets left, a considerable recovery given that many sage observers had suggested any sort of advantage would be difficult to create.

By the close in Hampshire, the home side had somehow extended their lead to 230, already a teak-tough chase when batting fourth. Their saviours had been James Vince and Abbott, this time with the bat. At the start of day three, Hampshire were eventually dismissed for 226, a lead of 280. However, such is the intrigue of four-day cricket, that the pitch seemed to be losing its demonic power once more and brows were starting to furrow at Chelmsford when Somerset reached 86/0. The BBC commentary team at Hampshire were suggesting Somerset would chase down the target.

At the same time, Essex were also taking control against Surrey with ten Doeschate completing a wonderful century under pressure, his fourth against The Oval outfit. From his first delivery, the Dutchman had flicked the ball to the leg side and scampered a rapid two, diving full length to beat Amal Virdi's throw. Eventually, 121 balls and 101 runs later, he mistimed a back cut and was caught at slip. As he went off, he spoke to incoming batsman Simon Harmer. One must surmise the instruction was 'bat carefully to get 350 and the fourth batting point, then throw everything at getting the fifth'. So began one of the most memorable mini-dramas of the season. Harmer did not score off his first 12 deliveries but having inched Essex to 350 from the first ball of the 103rd over, the South African let rip. He bashed seven fours and two sixes to complete a 46-ball half-century. It left Essex needing five runs from the last of the qualifying 110 overs to accumulate a full five batting points. However, to a great groan of disappointment, Sam Cook spooned a catch to Scott Borthwick from the first delivery. For the second successive game, Essex had missed a batting point at the death. Still, the home side led by 221 and the wearing pitch would only aid Harmer. Ten Doeschate waited only five overs of the Surrey second innings before introducing him at the River End.

There was always chatter among other county fans about the Chelmsford pitch being prepared for Harmer.

This game saw his 50th wicket of the Championship campaign on his home patch. However, Amar Virdi, who is ranked among England's brightest spinning prospects, only managed 3-116 from 32 overs when Essex batted. Though Harmer was wicketless in Surrey's first innings, in the second he took more than twice the number of wickets as Virdi for half the amount of runs. His 7-58 would be the ninth time he had recorded a five-for or better in 2019. The spinner had 78 wickets in the year and 207 in his three seasons since forgoing his international career with South Africa to become a Kolpak player with Essex.

The media were now starting to discuss the possibility of him qualifying for England. He could be eligible in 2020 and did little to quash the talk in the cricket media. However, the downside of stardom with England was demonstrated during the Surrey game when *The Sun* newspaper splashed with a story about the tragic family history of World Cup hero Ben Stokes. There was no justification, timeliness and contextual urgency, it was merely a juicy, salacious story. It was old school fare that I thought we'd gone beyond and was widely condemned by the cricketing community on Twitter.

As at Chelmsford, the Hampshire v Somerset match would begin sliding decisively towards Essex on day three. After a solid start, the visitors lost seven wickets for 14 runs before Dom Bess and Craig Overton offered late resistance. However, Abbott's second spell reaped 6-19 and overall match figures of 17-86 as Hampshire won by 136 runs. It was the fourth-best analysis in County Championship history and the best first-class match figures in England since Jim Laker's 19 for 90 against

Australia in the 1956 Ashes. Cheekily, he would be voted the Essex Player of the Month for September.

Afterwards, the bowler tweeted '@EssexCricket, you welcome'. Following a day like that, we could allow him some grammatical latitude.

The club's Championship season at Chelmsford concluded at 5.58pm on 18 September when Morne Morkel missed with a hefty swish and was bowled by Simon Harmer. For the first time in history, a county had won every home game. Only two of the seven had even reached the fourth day.

With one game left, Essex were 12 points clear of Somerset. Taking out the slim possibility of a strange set of bonus points, all the visitors had to do at Taunton next week was avoid defeat and they would win the County Championship.

But, between that game and this was the biggest party in domestic cricket.

'The death of a thousands nos'

17 September 2019, Some trendy diner in the West End of London

So I sat there at a job 'interview', nudging some rustic scrambled eggs around my plate and trying not to sell myself too desperately. My self-esteem had been slowly sinking under the 'death of a thousand nos' over the past few years. But I did not want to present myself as a pale imitation of the man I used to be and available at a knockdown price.

I was not sure I wanted this job. I just wanted someone to want me. I was more than qualified. My CV told a story of expertise and experience in equal measure. Of course, I had left off certain dates, such as my graduation from university. My chosen profession was one preferred by millennials more than the middle-aged. I surmised that recruiters could and would assume I was 21 or 22 when I graduated. From that, they could work out my age and probably pass me over. It should not be that way, in fact it is illegal in modern Britain. However, if we do not accept that everyone pre-judges ability based on appearance, then why had I turned up in a suit?

But for the experience of the previous three years, getting an interview would have been no surprise. I had been better suited for other roles and never received any sort of reply, not even an auto-response email. Recruiters were even worse. Salivating all over you one minute like a bad boyfriend then ghosting you the next like ... well ... a bad boyfriend.

This time I had a face-to-face 'pre-interview', which I presumed was really just about checking me out before they made me jump through all the HR hoops. That was fine by me. I had been on the other side of the interviewing process so many times in the previous decade. A colleague had once remarked: 'I decide in the first two minutes and so the remaining 28 are just about letting them leave with some sort of good grace.'

Given that the most HR-heavy organisations in which I had worked had also flouted their own rules in the worst ways when it suited them, I tended to think many interviews are like this.

We were eating breakfast in one of those American-style diners in the West End. It was just opposite the office of the interviewer but a long, hectic early-morning commute for me. This was just the start of the powerlessness I would feel that day.

The conversation flowed and I felt I performed well on this occasion. That was not always the case and, it may be a self-protection mechanism now, but I have long since assumed every interaction about any job would be a one-off. It was just easier that way. This time the conversation gave me some sort of hope. But a week later, I received feedback in which the only really meaningful phrase was 'he thought you were overqualified'. I had heard that previously, along with other crackers such as 'we think you have done this all before'. It all smacked of ageism to me. They sat there and thought 'do we really want this fat, grey bloke managing our young and vibrant team?' Of course 'cultural fit' is a real issue but I have always found competence and experience circumvents all that.

You have to bear in mind that you are being compared to others and there can be only one winner. Those are the rules. These no-names might be good, very good in fact and that should not undermine any faith in your abilities. Then again, there is always the nagging possibility of another reason. The modern term is imposter syndrome but that's just a fancy name for good old-fashioned insecurity. Even in a long and seemingly successful career there is always the troubling feeling that you have been winging it all along thanks to a few lucky breaks at the right time. However, when the chips were down you just could not cut it. You know all those meetings years ago where you felt a little lost? Yes, as you suspected at the time, everyone really was better than you. Persistent rejection over time allows the devil on your shoulder to outshout the angel whispering platitudes on the other side.

A person in my situation with a glass-half-empty disposition would beat themselves up over any lethargy, inadequacy or failure. But to be fair to myself, I had worked very hard, trying to nudge the edges of my potential and taken major career risks. That is exactly what the gurus advise, right? Perhaps this was just 'entitlement' by another name. I was merely a pale, stale, lower-middle class male blinking at the light of the bright future that lay directly behind me. We had a chat about a decent job. For once, I thought I did well. I tried to put it out of my head immediately but, as when you find a house you wish to buy, it is impossible to stop imagining a life there. You think about the route to work, the fun, benefits and the positive contribution you could create. That all stopped midway through day two of Essex v Surrey when, as I watched ten Doeschate approach his century from in front of the pavilion, I got a call from an unknown number. I picked up the message, walked off toward the nets behind the building and rang back the recruiter. He then informed me that I was so damn qualified for this particular role they had no intention of employing me to do it.

I sank a little lower in my chair that afternoon as Essex piled up the runs and vowed to return the next day.

Twenty20 Finals Day
(and the important apology)

Edgbaston, 21 September 2019

AROUND 10PM under the blazing lights of an effervescent Edgbaston, Simon Harmer somehow squeezed a delivery from Wayne Parnell towards cover point. As soon as the ball beat the sprawling dive of the Worcestershire fielder, we knew the Vitality Blast Trophy belonged to Essex for the first time. It had been a hell of a journey.

The team had taken a meandering, sometimes tortuous route to the showpiece game. It started sluggishly, with a combination of ineptitude and rain bringing them just two wins from their first ten games. There was rumoured to be rancour in the ranks before they found the formula for a stunning late charge through the qualification stages. In the quarter-final, they beat a group-topping yet geographically displaced Lancashire side on a bitterly cold evening in Durham thanks to a thunderous late assault from Ravi Bopara. Ahead of Finals Day, the language of the Essex hierarchy was illuminating. Whether it was to galvanise team spirit or they really believed it, senior figures spoke about this 'small club' battling against the big boys of the county game.

OK, you could argue the divide between Test and non-Test grounds had been ever more pronounced since the announcement of The Hundred. And yes, Chelmsford was a tough proposition on Twenty20 nights but, even filled to bursting, its 7,000 capacity represented a third of the spectators required to pack out Lord's or The Oval. But, at the same time, away games hardly felt like little Frodo travelling into Mordor to take on Sauron and his armies either.

My route to Edgbaston today seemed to go through the heart of Tolkien's 'Shire' at one stage. The previous week's trip to the Midlands had warned me off the M1/M6 roadworks and going south through the centre of Birmingham on a Saturday seemed to be asking for trouble. So I meandered through that picture-book part of Buckinghamshire that links the A40 to the M40. However, my quest to see Essex lift ... ahem ... 'the precious' would be interrupted by a loud pop in the fast lane of the M40 around Banbury.

A dour yet highly efficient RAC repairman replaced my flat tyre and sent me on my way. However, for 90 frustrating minutes, I was sitting on a deckchair high on the grassy verge reading the paper, watching the cars whizz past and listening to Worcestershire Rapids pile up a sizeable total against Nottinghamshire Outlaws in the first semi-final. Initially, they had told me no repairman would reach me before Essex started their semi-final. If you added the remaining journey time plus parking and walking then my side might be as good as out when I finally got to the ground. In the end, it seemed to be an all-too-familiar customer service ploy that meant the eventual one-and-a-half-hour wait would be treated with grateful salvation. But whatever the psychological shenanigans, my grand plan was in tatters.

The idea had been to pace myself by arriving midway through the opening game. It was my third tactic for my third visit to Twenty20 Finals Day. The others had ended dismally. At Trent Bridge in 2006, Essex lost to the canniness of Paul Nixon's Leicestershire in the opening game. They were not the first to fall prey to the wily old Foxes, who would go on to lift their second title in three years. But I recall looking ahead to the rest of the day in glum disappointment. I missed the second semi to buy a jumper and woolly hat because I'd arrived utterly underdressed for a surprisingly chilly August day. Then I arrived back to the ground to watch the Sugababes perform a thoroughly disinterested set at the interval. I shivered through a tense final that meant little to me on a largely miserable day.

It was little better at Hampshire in 2010. Again Essex were up first, this time against the hosts so I hurtled down the M3 in the hope of a match-winning effort from hard-hitting West Indian all-rounder Dwayne Bravo. Despite finishing second in the South Group with a decent record then dispatching Lancashire with something to spare in the quarter-final, Essex had decided to spend a sum that would reportedly wipe out their entire profit in the competition on 'a ringer' for Finals Day. Bravo lasted eight balls before being run out on five and his four overs cost 46 runs. By the time he got his only wicket, Hampshire were well on the way to victory. Dispirited and well aware of the long, passion-free day coming up, I jumped in my car and was home in time to watch the final on television. Forewarned and forearmed, I thought I would take it steady this time. By arriving midway through the first game, I could watch Essex and still be fresh enough for the final, whoever got there. It would shorten one of the longest days in UK spectator sport.

However, my burst tyre meant I reached the first matchday car park with Essex batting deep into their opening powerplay. I was asked for £20 and assured by a woman who had lost most of her front teeth and almost all of her civility that this school playing field represented the only spaces still available. I promptly turned around, found a nearby road in which to park and called an Uber. It cost me £4.50 and saved me a two-mile walk plus an extra 20 minutes in getting to the ground.

When you are late to a sold-out sporting event, someone will have sat in your seat. When you challenge them, they will say 'No one is in their right seats, mate.' It is almost a legal requirement. For all I know it is part of the small print on the back of the ticket. This came to pass. My approach was to sit in the nearest free seat and declare that when the owner wanted their rightful place back, I would be looking for mine. This practice of putting the onus on the other person and waiting often does the trick.

I was at the very top of the West Stand. The walk up would get more tedious as the day went on but the view was always spectacular. The rumour was that each competing club had been given 750 tickets once their attendance on Finals Day was assured. The Essex allocation sold out within a few hours. We were all together but, as we later found out, next to blocks of Derbyshire and Worcestershire fans.

As I have already discussed, Twenty20 is the format I least enjoy watching live. The cricket itself is enthralling but the crowds are drunken, boorish and, after a few pints, can horribly overestimate their humorous capacity. The popularity of the games prevents you from moving seats to escape their antics or avoid hearing the quite incredible conversations that inebriated fans, often in fancy dress, are prepared to air in public.

Deep into the Essex run-chase against Worcestershire, 'Thor' and the 'Hulk' were loudly discussing the issues surrounding IVF treatment in the row behind me. They had already covered planning law and how to efficiently build an extension while Moeen Ali was steering the Rapids towards a handy score.

'Mate, mate, maaaaate,' implored the drunken Norse God to his green friend at one point. 'It is not as easy as you think to get pregnant.'

Talking loudly while ... well ... hammered is no crime and given their intoxication they were reasonably well behaved, although my ears did prick up when a man behind me shouted 'Send them home' at the dismissal of Moeen Ali. No one can be sure if it was racially motivated and certainly it was the only such comment I heard all day. It was one sentence uttered by a man who, in that moment, was under the influence of too much alcohol and too little common sense. But these are troubling times and words have always been able to open wounds, mentally and physically. Added to that, Moeen Ali plays for England. He is an admirable player whose achievements have been based on hard work and humility. We need more like him.

While the Twenty20 revolution has been a huge, worldwide success, it is widely acknowledged that the alcohol-fuelled antics of its UK crowds have put off many people, especially those with families, from coming to a form of cricket that surely would be the most enticing to a younger audience. I have tried desperately to get my children to follow cricket and the fast-paced nature of Twenty20 is the brightest attraction. Essex used to host some Sunday games in the early days of the competition and I sat with a gaggle of parents on the grass in front of the pavilion on a couple of lazy afternoons. These occasions had a relaxed 'village green' feel, though I recall frantically shielding my entire family as a vicious sweep shot from Mark Pettini caused spectators to scatter.

As the competition developed, Friday night fixtures began to dominate Twenty20 and rare Sunday games were marketed as 'Family Days'. This implied, deliberately or not, that the remaining games were focused on others. Fridays nearly always sold out at Chelmsford and, presumably, alcohol sales provided a big boost to the coffers. Given the parlous state of the county finances, you cannot argue with the business sense but many of my age and sensibility simply followed Twenty20 on the television. In addition, the games were outside of the scope of the membership and the prospect of paying an extra £25 per game to be sardined in and then sung at by football fans really started to wane as I got older.

Essex had set up their last-gasp qualification from the South Group of this year's Vitality Blast thanks to a ten-run victory over Kent on the last Friday night in August. During a break in play, a male streaker raced to the middle, ran up to the stumps and, stooping down, knocked the bails off with his genitals. This may have enshrined his status as 'a total, bloody nutter' down the pub, but I'd venture his lasting legacy will be as a slide in an ECB presentation arguing Twenty20 will not bring families or children back to the game. In fairness to The Hundred, which in case you have been speed-reading this book I think is an appalling idea, cheap family tickets and 'policies' on alcohol consumption were being rumoured as part of a push to alter the audience to short-form cricket in the UK. This aspect is welcome.

I have watched sport all over the world, Olympics 100m final, Champions League Final, major football games in the US and Asia, yet Twenty20 Finals Day is the longest event I have ever attended. Quite understandably, it is a party for most and, as usual at Edgbaston, the Hollies Stand took centre stage. As the day and the drink wore on various fancy dress groups were running up and down its steps being chased by others. My favourites included huntsmen in pursuit of a fox and a swarm of bees tracking what appeared to be marshmallows. While hardly exclusive to these shores, I do enjoy the stereotypical English eccentricity of it all.

But, inevitably, those who start the party early are flagging by the final game. They are up and out of their seats for beer, the toilet, a walk, more beer, more toilet breaks. I was on the end of a row with fans seemingly suffering from a potent combination of raging thirst, small bladder syndrome and ADHD. Therefore I spent the last hours of Finals Day bobbing up and down like a buoy in the shipping lane.

However, they were still relatively sober when I finally arrived at Edgbaston around 3pm, midway through the

Essex domination of Derbyshire in the second semi-final. Walking into the ground after my nightmare journey, I heard the PA announce the demise of Cameron Delport. But his belligerent 55 off 31 balls had set the platform for a competitive total. The rest of the innings did not quite match the start but Tom Westley, Bopara and Adam Wheater all contributed to a total of 160/5. Given that Nottinghamshire had failed to overturn Worcestershire's 147 in the first semi-final, the Essex fans were relatively optimistic.

Delport would be the only overseas star for Essex on Finals Day; the other two places were left unfilled. Pakistani paceman Mohammad Amir had returned home before the quarter-final against Lancashire and Essex would be without Adam Zampa for the first time today. Like all the Australian tourists, he was back Down Under after a long summer in England. Though he had not been a stand-out performer, the leg-break bowler was excellent in stunting the offensive intentions of opposition batsmen during key periods. The failure to fill either of the last two spots brought some grumbling from the Essex supporters and the club did try to find replacements. Perhaps memories of the Bravo experience still lingered.

However, the Edgbaston wicket was slow and Harmer needed a spin partner. In came Aron Nijjar, a slow left-arm bowler from Ilford, a place that had previously provided Essex and England captains Graham Gooch and Nasser Hussain. Nijjar, by contrast, was 24 and had played just one Twenty20 game in his short career. Like many spinners, his action had its eccentricities, clasping his palms together on the ball early in the run then throwing both hands in the air on approach.

When his first four balls in the Derbyshire reply went 4,6,0,4, I feared he would be hit out of the attack but his fifth was fired in more quickly and clipped the top of Wayne Madsen's leg stump. It felt like a key moment, not just because of the South African's renowned batting ability but it gave the young bowler crucial belief. Nijjar ended up with a highly creditable 3-26. Harmer, who bowled Billy Godleman with his first ball, took his standard, stellar 4-19. Even the part-time spin of Dan Lawrence, whose front-on action had more peccadillos than Nijjar's, was also a potent weapon, taking 1-20 in three overs. Essex gradually squeezed the life out of the Derbyshire run-chase. They were dismissed for 126 with eight balls remaining. Against all the odds, my team had reached their first Twenty20 final.

The break before the big one was a chance to catch my breath and savour the atmosphere of an occasion that has quickly become a highlight on the UK sporting calendar. Finals Day had grown in stature and confidence since I last attended. It was more of a US-style 'experience' with sponsor activations and a wider variety of food options. I don't remember vegan food stalls, three bands playing simultaneously in different parts of the venue and a mini fun-fair at the Rose Bowl all those years ago.

However, as usual, the best fun was crowd-created, such as watching the mini-cricket games begin to take shape. The scenario is always the same. Two or three children, most often boys in their young teens, find a scrap of space for a game that shatters all the important health and safety regulations in the UK. The one I watched form was on a patch of grass by a supermarket over the road from Edgbaston where spectators were picnicking. The 'strip' was eight yards long and the field an unusual, yet attacking 0-1 off-side set-up. They biffed the ball around for two minutes, darting dangerously between those standing or sitting nearby, avoiding all manner of alcohol, pies and pastries strewn on rugs. It is something no one would tolerate in normal life but this is a much-loved festival day on the sporting calendar. After a while, men, and it is nearly always men, drifted over, stood smiling for a while and got themselves involved. Their enthusiasm was limitless and yet they realised the children must remain the stars. They are the equivalent of net bowlers but undoubtedly they got the most from the game.

By now, the whole affair was getting bigger and the noise emanating had increased. The ball was biffed further and the boys, especially the middle-aged ones, pushed out the parameters of the outfield. Even really old boys, by that I mean septuagenarians, seemed keen to get involved. When an onside slog went his way, one pensioner eased to his feet on arthritic knees, stretched down to collect the ball and then, with concentration suggesting they wanted to prove they 'used to play a bit', hurled it back in the general direction of the bowler.

This scene was much more entertaining than the 'special guest' the PA announcer had promised before the break. Clearly, the appearance of Mr Motivator, a '90s TV fitness personality, was linked with the sponsor of the competition. So were the garish pink headbands many were sporting on the day. I was happy to give both a miss. The opposite could be said of the other major 'set-piece' – the Mascot Race. It was a Twenty20 tradition and always raised a smile. Unfortunately I had heard this year's event on the radio as my car hobbled towards Birmingham.

After clambering back up to the top of the West Stand ahead of the final, I noted that few fans had left. This seemed to be a contrast to the occasions in which Essex had been dumped out early. Maybe that was because most tickets were sold to non-affiliated fans before the competing teams were known. Or perhaps, it was that the 'event' was just more compelling these days. All the fan engagement tricks were employed, music blaring out between balls, fireworks, T-shirt cannons, big screenshots of spectators between overs with KissCam, SimbaCam. The announcer even claimed that the Ba-Ba-Baaaaaaaaaa sing-song to 'Sweet Caroline' 'started on Twenty20 Finals Day'. For me, that is a highly dubious honour but, undoubtedly, this format has both swollen county coffers and grown the appeal of the game. If you had to suffer a few sweaty, emotional blokes singing Neil Diamond in your ear at 9pm on a September evening in Birmingham in order to see Essex lift a trophy that was a small price to pay.

Like most county fans, I had liked the shortest format straightaway but, unlike some, always saw it as legitimate cricket. Grant Flower was a shy man but a highly effective all-rounder for Essex, especially in Twenty20 with his miserly, nagging spin. Interviewing him for the club website after one man-of-the-match performance, I remarked that he had 'just taken his maiden hat-trick in top-class cricket'. He immediately smiled and gently responded that 'This is not top-class cricket.' Given that an increasing number of players are retiring from the red-ball game to concentrate on the shorter versions few would agree now.

Whatever the merits of the format, Twenty20 Finals day was now firmly established as 'English cricket's day out'. Like the Gillette Cup finals of the 1970s, 80s and 90s, only better. As usual in cricket, there were a host of variables affecting the play. Firstly there was the precipitation problem. A heavy dew had always been considered a big factor in the Gillette Cup Final and the toss often felt decisive. Likewise, batting in twilight with the onset of evening moisture is an important factor on Twenty20 Finals Day too but perhaps it was not quite so conclusive.

Then again, the game seemed to have made major technical advancements since its shortest version had been invented. One of cricket's ongoing fascinations is the equilibrium between the forces of bat and ball. Innovation has never allowed the balance to stay static for long and Twenty20 was the ultimate illustration. 'Impossible' runchases full of frying pan shots and reverse sweeps seemed standard just a couple of years later, as did gymnastic tagteam fielding and specialist 'death bowlers' able to stifle batsmen with precise yorkers.

It was hard to see a direct link between the staid, whiteclothed Gillette Cup finals of my early youth, televised by the BBC and hosted by Peter West, and the all-action, multi-coloured Twenty20 Blast, fronted by the eccentric David 'Bumble' Lloyd. Yet the evolution was moving still further. Whether you like The Hundred or not, it would be impossible to ignore. Changes to the county schedule would mean the 50-over final would be moved away from Lord's next season so those famous balcony shots at the pavilion would not be repeated. Meanwhile, the rumoured marketing budget and remodelled schedule surrounding The Hundred had to subtract something from the Twenty20 event next year. So this one felt a little special.

Surprisingly, Harmer switched tactics for the final. He won the toss and elected to chase. The skipper revealed afterwards that the dew was a factor in this thinking. Many thought it was a mistake and said so on Twitter. Meanwhile, Porter was replaced by Cook, who would be playing his first Twenty20 game of the season. Nijjar was only playing his second and Essex had arrived without two of the overseas stars that shone in the latter Group Stages. In addition, Worcester were holders and Twenty20 specialists. Essex were up against it.

Spin would dominate the final. A fact illustrated when batsman Lawrence, a part-time practitioner at best, opened the bowling and his first ball turned almost 45 degrees after pitching just outside off stump and was called for a clear wide. Lawrence's second legal ball was edged through the slips and the next pitched on middle before ripping off the turf to hit the top of Hamish Rutherford's off stump. Clearly, the strip was still slow but turning sharply. The clever approach seemed to be to bat cautiously, attacking the seamers and milking what you could off the spinners. This is exactly the opposite of the prevailing one-day tactics two decades ago. Wheater stood up to the stumps to prevent the openers dancing down the track to Sam Cook but he still went for 19 off his first 10 balls.

Worcestershire were progressing nicely at 7.5 runs per over before Harmer induced the gentlest of return catches from dangerman Moeen Ali midway through the ninth over to make it 61/2. The South African got a somewhat fortunate lbw decision against Ben Cox next ball and had a solid if unsuccessful shout for a hat-trick against Parnell. After beating his bat on numerous occasions, Harmer would eventually bowl the left-hander with the penultimate ball of his allotted four overs to reduce Worcestershire to 90/4.

The skipper nearly pulled off a full-length diving catch on the boundary to see the end of Riki Wessels at the start of the 15th over. The opener had accumulated a run-a-ball 31 and was anchoring the innings skilfully. Two balls later he pushed a quick single into the covers and Paul Walters threw down the stumps. There seemed little alarm but the umpires checked with the TV replay anyway. When the video referee assessed the footage on the big screen, players and fans suddenly erupted. Wessels was run out, fractionally but clearly. Had the Australian-born right-hander stayed for longer the Worcestershire middle order would have been able to launch a more aggressive assault at the death.

Approaching the final overs, it was still hard to gauge the state of the game. Essex had kept the run-rate around seven per over and taken a wicket or two more than Worcestershire would have liked. However, the pitch always seemed better for setting than chasing.

As ever, the crowd was the best barometer and, around now, a section of the Worcestershire fans were confident enough to stand up in unison and sing their songs directly at the Essex fans. However, Harmer was still mixing up his bowlers so their team never quite got away. Though the decision to hand the 18th over to Delport surprised many, he conceded just ten runs and a back-of-the-hand delivery saw Ross Whiteley caught in the deep. Nijjar only allowed five runs off the 19th and four byes at the start of the 20th helped Worcester reach 145/9 at the close. It seemed pretty much par. Between innings, I tried to put the upcoming chase into context on Twitter. 'If EssexCricket win the

VitalityBlast, I'd argue it is the biggest comeback in our history. Remember, we were dead and buried before the last half-dozen group games. Can't think of a run like that before, can you? Not that this is done. But we restricted them to a gettable score.'

Throughout the day, the elderly lady sitting next to me had been periodically muttering in my ear. She clearly wanted to chat but I struggled to engage due to my natural reserve and the fact that her comments were a little inane. For example, when Worcestershire were 82/3 off 11 overs, she leant over and said: 'It would be great to keep them under 100, wouldn't it?' I replied with platitudes and smiles but did not really converse. Of course, this runs contrary to the 'be kind' mantra of which many, including me, prescribe. From her canary yellow kit and array of badges it was clear she was a passionate Essex fan, exactly the type of supporter with whom I engaged so energetically on social media. It seemed that, for both of us, real life was the problem. When I came back after the long break between the semi-final and final and saw she had not moved, it was clear she was on her own today, physically and emotionally. It must have taken a lot of money, time and energy for her to be there. I should have talked to her more, asked a question or two and met her more than halfway. I just should have done better. Apologies.

Whether the late evening dew was settling or not, it was clear from the opening over, when Delport's attempted sweep off Moeen Ali hit the cue-end of the bat, that the pitch would be a pudding all night. The first seven balls produced just one run and, from then on, the Essex chase always felt like it was trailing by half a dozen runs. Especially when the same South African, whose belligerence so often set up a decent total, was caught on the midwicket boundary off the 14th ball with the score on nine. It showed the importance of scoreboard pressure even in the early stages of an innings. He had been in for seven balls and scored just one. After six overs, Essex were 36/1. By some margin, it was the lowest opening powerplay of the day and there was mumbling of concern in the stand around me. However, my yardstick in run-chases is always the Duckworth–Lewis–Stern score (DLS). Although this formula was calculated by mathematicians to determine the winner in games truncated by rain, it serves as an excellent all-weather guide to who has their noses in front. Despite a little despondency among the Essex fans, the DLS suggested the chase was always nicely in touch.

Westley and Wheater rebuilt the innings diligently but gradually the scoreboard began to nag again. The latter had perished, disappointingly bowled around his legs trying to reverse sweep. When the former was caught for 36 by a sliding Pat Brown at deep square leg, Essex were 65/3 and needing 81 off 57 balls. By the time Lawrence holed out to join ten Doeschate back in the pavilion that equation was down to 64 off 42 with five wickets left.

The next three overs would be Ravi Bopara's key contribution. He thrashed two fours and two sixes as Essex plundered 30 runs, just about on the run-rate. However, Walter was struggling to connect and his strike-rate was less than a run per ball. From the third delivery of Brown's final over, the 19th of the innings, he finally slapped a boundary. However, with 17 now needed from nine deliveries, his wicket from the next ball might have been a necessary evil as the hard-hitting Harmer seemed better suited for the finale. The skipper thumped a four over the bowler's head from his first ball and then scythed a single from the final delivery to keep the strike. Bopara, the potential match-winner with 35 off 21 deliveries, was stranded at the other end. Parnell had been the hero of the first semi-final by restricting Nottinghamshire to seven runs from the last over. He seemed set to repeat the trick when Essex, needing 12, could only manage singles from their first two deliveries. Then Harmer swiped twos from the third and fourth. Again the in-form, well-set Bopara was at the non-striker's end and now the Eagles required six from two balls to win.

Then the game changed.

Until now, Worcestershire had always seemed to be leading. Not by much but enough. However, from the penultimate ball, Harmer repeated his stand-and-swipe shot over the bowler's head for four. Before it had even bounced, Parnell bent over and put his head in his hands. He seemed physically and mentally shattered, so much so that captain Moeen Ali went over to revive his spirits. Even from my vantage point high in the stands, it was clear Parnell had unravelled. I could not understand his reaction given that a dot ball or a wicket would see Worcestershire retain their title and his story would be written as a comeback, not a choke.

Parnell is an excellent all-rounder, with vast Twenty20 experience in the Indian Premier League, the Caribbean Premier League, English county cricket and Test matches for South Africa. But, for me, he buckled, publicly and quite unnecessarily, to give Essex a crucial advantage. His final ball was straight and full but far from the yorker required. Harmer angled his bat and squirted a shot to the boundary. Seconds later, a batch of red fireworks flew into the sky from either side of the City End.

Harmer raced towards the square leg boundary, flung his arms out wide and was embraced by his jubilant team-mates. This was 'the moment'. It was his moment, the team's moment, the club's moment and the supporters' moment. And it was my moment too. The moment that was worth all the money, time and attention throughout the season. Let alone the kitchen sink drama of my day.

I videoed the final ball on my phone but there was no need, the snapshot in my brain will always remember that elation. Unlike almost all County Championship or Test victories, this was an explosive conclusion to a game played on a knife-edge throughout. Squeezing that shot through the infield will be seen as inevitable when the story is retold or the video rewatched, but it was not. Had Harmer not beaten the fielder, there would have been recriminations about his decision to field first, the lack of an overseas bowler and, in general, about the fortune that Essex enjoyed to make Finals Day anyway. However, history is written by the winners.

It was noticeable that Bopara did not race to join in the celebrations. Instead, he casually took off his helmet and gloves then sauntered towards the throbbing mass of Essex players celebrating on the square leg boundary. It is dangerous and near impossible to extrapolate an athlete's longer-term thoughts and emotions from their body language in the moment. Fans and journalists are often guilty of 'X must mean Y' causality when it is just a correlation at that second. Reporters spoke of Bopara's coolness under pressure, something he had displayed with crucial, conspicuous boundary-hitting throughout the late Essex charge towards the trophy. A meme of Bopara producing a knowing wink into the camera as he walked off the pitch did the rounds on social media shortly after the final. Someone slowed it down and added emotional, almost sexy, music. It all added to the feeling Bopara was utterly in control and clear-headed.

In fact, you could argue the opposite. During the group campaign, there were suggestions that Bopara was unhappy to be dropped down to No 6 in the batting order. He had been left out for a couple of group games, reportedly after disagreeing with the decision. His return was dramatic and pivotal, scoring 45, 14, 70*, 47*, 39*, 27 and 36* in his last seven innings of the Vitality Blast at rates that either won games outright or turned them unequivocally in Essex's favour.

So, a decision that he passionately, vocally opposed had helped turn around his form and that of the team, unexpectedly transforming them both into winners. You can understand it if his emotions were slightly mixed. At the close of the season, with two winners' medals still hanging around his neck rumours spread that Bopara would be leaving Chelmsford; he wanted to concentrate on white-ball cricket. While he had been a heavy run-scorer and useful bowler in all short forms for years, you could argue his late, triumphant but perhaps unhappy form had added to his marketability. Less than a month after 'that night' at Edgbaston, it was announced that Bopara was ending his 18-year association with Essex and moving to Sussex.

Perhaps a subtle power shift was indicated by the elevation of 'Harmy Army' above 'Oh Ravi Bopara' as the Essex fans' song of the night. They belted out the former as the ground quickly emptied. The number of neutrals and the long day meant only a couple of pockets of Eagles supporters remained for the trophy-lift and, annoyingly, even that was made towards the virtually empty main stand. It was all arranged for television, of course, but my view was less than side on and those Essex fans at the City End only knew Harmer had lifted the trophy when plumes of ticker tape flew up over the back of the stage.

One of the most convivial qualities of county cricket is that success can be properly shared. Players are prepared to go over to fans for hugs, handshakes and selfies. Often they initially wander over to talk to family and club-mates only to get collared by the general public. But, almost always, they are tolerant and, frankly, just nice about it. The Essex team took the loving embrace of the West Stand before going over to the City End group. As ever, I planned this badly. By the time I had moved down from on high to the first group the players had moved on and then, by the time I followed on, they had virtually finished. But then, I am uncomfortable in the role of a fanboy, if that term exists for someone so deep into middle age. Selfies feel almost insufferable to me and I detest the awkwardness of asking.

By the time I'd scampered around to the City End most of the players had moved on. Bopara lingered longest, agreeing to every request. Beaming down on the scene from an executive box was Ronnie Irani. How the former Essex captain, now chairman, would have loved the attention and buzz of victory at Twenty20 Finals Day. A loveable, vocal but sometimes irascible character, his return to Essex had ushered in the appointment of head coach Chris Silverwood, then his replacement Anthony McGrath and ten Doeschate, two people upon which the club's recent red-ball success was based. Now they had a white-ball trophy too. After grabbing their selfies, the Essex fans gradually slipped away. Not wanting the moment to pass, I lingered far too long.

Empty sports stadiums are strange places, especially when the quiet of the night descends so quickly after the drama and excitement. When I finally left, I was met with the perverse sight of an inebriated man dressed as a ninja turtle drawing deeply on a cigarette and swaying gently as he peered inquisitively into his phone. Then I passed a bevvy of irate superheroes trying and failing to summon a taxi.

By now it was very late, very dark and I had a very long, slow journey ahead of me. My spare tyre would only suffer speeds of 50mph so I was expecting to be on the road for over three hours. I walked back the mile to my car alone. I had to. I had come on my own and barring a couple of texts and my stilted conversation with the lady next to me, I had interacted with virtually no one. This had been one of the best days of my Essex-supporting life but, frankly, the rest of my world did not care. I tweeted throughout, liking, replying and conversing with a host of people. But this was a time for real not virtual companionship.

I stopped for petrol, loaded up with celebratory, diet-smashing chocolate and set the sat nav to home. My eyes were moist by the time I'd reached the motorway. Sporting success for my teams always brings a strange, incongruent melancholy. Partly it is the release of pent-up anxiety, but mostly because it makes me think about my father. My sporting preferences are almost entirely shaped by him. In truth, he was a distinctly average man, and I have always wanted to be something more. I blame a sliver, but only a sliver, of my own failures on gaps in the guidance he gave, the acceptance of the mediocre, the ill discipline and the general failure to break out of a narrow life. It was killing me that, as I got older, I was starting to look, sound and act more like him. Still, he was a thoroughly decent man, with compassion and a moral compass that he had successfully passed on. He had also loved Essex County Cricket Club.

On that long, slow, dark drive home I thought about him and I cried.

Somerset v Essex (and the idiot)

Taunton, 25 September 2019

'GOING TO the cricket?' said the woman pushing a trolley of efficiently stacked yet staggeringly overpriced snacks through the 9.02 from Paddington.

The elderly man at the adjacent table grunted affirmatively. We had been on the train for 45 minutes and it was the first indication that he was off to the Championship decider too. Despite my Essex hat on the table, we had sat solo and silent, as if we were at the Hayes Close End at Chelmsford.

Taunton was a new ground for me. It was over £100 for an open return on the train but it was a quick journey with only a handful of stops, plus the distance between the station and ground looked like a ten-minute walk. From the platform at Paddington to my seat in the stand was about two hours. Thanks to London Transport's inability to cope with rain, the duration from Paddington to my living room on the way back would be almost as long. But then the weather was foul and, unfortunately, would taint this historic game.

Somerset's defeat at Hampshire meant they were 12 points behind Essex; therefore, they would be preparing 'a result pitch' for Jack Leach and their other spinners. With rain likely to restrict playing time to an aggregate of two days from a possible four, it was set to be a minefield for batsmen. So it proved.

Somerset were 75/4 at the end of a soggy day one restricted to less than 28 overs. The game moved on only a little further on day two, with Roelof van der Merwe hitting 60 off 51 balls and sharing a last-wicket partnership with Leach (11) to haul Somerset up to 203 all out. Around 180 was being touted as the minimum required for the hosts to be 'in the game' and Harmer's 5-105 revealed all you need to know about the pitch. Still, Alastair Cook and Nick Browne skilfully navigated the final overs and Essex were 25/0 at the close.

I had chosen to go on day three as the weather forecast suggested it would see the most play. I hoped to stay over for the conclusion too. After a damp start, it was forecast to clear up but it was no surprise to see angled raindrops on the carriage window as we flew through Wiltshire and arrowed deep into the cider county. There was a steady stream of grey men with rucksacks and rain jackets as I got off at Taunton. I followed them to the ground. On the way, I passed an old-fashioned record shop taking up a shard of space in the main street. It was open for business but you could not tell. It was rundown and ramshackle. There was what my parents would have called 'a gramophone' in the window, alongside 'a record player' that must have started life playing Freddie and the Dreamers or Herman's Hermits. It might advertise itself as 'vintage' and 'for connoisseurs only'. In fact, it was just old. I wondered how it made any money to stay open. Of course, the irony was not lost on me given I had travelled 200 miles to sit in the rain and see a sport accused of exactly the same problem.

The start was delayed so I went into a café in a supermarket alongside the ground to top up my caffeine. Then, after more rain, I secured my stay with a stodgy meal. It turned out to be the most English of days – full of warm drinks, attending a sporting event in hope more than expectation, rain and talking about rain. In the supermarket, a Somerset supporter engaged me in conversation at one point and Brexit even popped up. He saw I was streaming Question Time as Prime Minister Boris Johnson was returning to MPs' scrutiny for the first time after his prorogation of Parliament had been ruled illegal.

In the afternoon with weather relenting, I entered the County Ground, Somerset for the first time. As usual, there was a mixture of the old and new, the corporate and the fan-centric. Remembrances were retained in the artwork, murals and landmarks, such as the Joel Garner gates. I especially liked the space retained for traditional benches, each with a plaque portraying a sporting life spent idling at the boundary edge. One read: 'In memory of Dad, who loved his days here, missed by us all and forever in our hearts.' Another talked of: 'A loving family man who spent many happy hours watching and helping Somerset County Cricket Club.' These people were in their prime when that record player was still relevant but it felt right to preserve their memories. They were the lifeblood of the club, the people who had fallen in love with the game at Taunton.

No Somerset supporter, alive or dead, had seen their side win the County Championship. Undoubtedly, the biggest story was the home side finally landing that elusive first title. In addition, Marcus Trescothick would be leaving the county at the end of the campaign after 27 seasons on the books. Victory would be a fitting farewell for a player who served his county and country so proudly, even breaking boundaries with his honest portrayal of his mental health issues at a time when it was not trendy or easy to do so. A 'virus' and then the euphemism of 'stress-related illness' were used at the time to describe his absences from the England team on tour. However, you knew that certain people within the game would be suggesting privately it was a weakness to be exploited. Despite all the fine work going on, society often acts as though it is, even though it publicly professes to the contrary.

Barring a late appearance on the field as 12th man on the final day Trescothick did not feature in this game but you could feel his presence throughout, especially in the media. This was entirely understandable, though it did rankle to endlessly discuss Somerset's and Trescothick's loss rather than the Essex victory in the immediate aftermath. However, the most irritating aspect of the entire four days was Sky rolling out its Kevin Pietersen documentary in instalments during the rain breaks in the television coverage. We can all handle filler content in these gaps but Trescothick's humility and respect for all areas of cricket stood in stark contrast to the former's self-importance. I would have rather watched the 43-year-old Somerset legend in the indoor nets all day than be subjected to any more of KP's indestructible ego.

Meanwhile, my day was starting to look bleak. The umpires went out to inspect the pitch following a prolonged dry spell after lunch and it promptly started raining down on them. A 3.20pm inspection only led to the announcement of another at 4.30pm. Grumbles and 'get-on-with-it' type shouts from the stands greeted the umpires' every appearance. The crowd was sparse but then the locals had the luxury of looking at the forecast before venturing in. The Essex fans had to sit it out. The only respite from watching the rain came from a group of university students who drank some beer and sang some songs, football-style.

When it was announced that play was called off for the day, the locals formed an orderly queue at the ticket office for refunds and I made my way back to the station. Regretfully, commitments at home and my lack of planning meant I could not stay over for the final day. As it turned out, I would miss the key moment of a Championship-winning season yet again. Bar Headingley, I had been to a day of every away game, including the season-opening friendly at Cambridge University, yet I would miss the special moment. But then, no one really expected the final day to be quite so enthralling.

The opening 38 overs were quiet enough. Essex only lost Browne and, despite turn and uneven bounce from the pitch, the visitors had some measure of comfort. Cook had survived an early lbw appeal when replays suggested he was out. It would become a pivotal moment. A 2011 study by Douglas Miller suggested county captains were less likely to be given out by umpires than other players. He argued it was unconscious bias given the skipper would submit a report on the official at the end of the game.

Cook was not a captain but he was the key wicket and had the finger been raised the visitors could not have complained. The moment has drawn scrutiny because Essex would capitulate when he was caught in the slips off Leach with the score on 102. However, replays proved Jack Leach was also lbw when Somerset were 163/9, a decision that would cost Essex 40 crucial runs.

Essex would lose their final nine wickets for 39 runs in less than 19 overs. Somerset had a sniff of a chance. Afterwards, Cook revealed that, following his first dismissal, he was certain he would bat again that day. Time constraints meant Somerset had to forfeit their second innings. Essex needed 63 to win but, realistically, it was about batting out time.

Their first innings had finished at 4.16pm. From 4.30pm, there would be only one hour of cricket left in the season. It was a minimum of 16 overs but with Somerset bowling spinners they might squeeze in 20.

It was a long shot but you only had to look back at the previous hour to realise the importance of momentum. The pitch had started spinning on day one but, in terms of overs bowled, this was only day two. Ten Doeschate asked for the light roller between innings – it seemed to settle down most of those early inconsistencies. Cook and Browne looked as solid as any Essex pair all day. They also punished any loose delivery which, by the virtue of an ultra-attacking field, often produced a boundary.

Trescothick came on as 12th man and crowded around the bat with Essex 38/0 at the start of the 16th over. Two balls later, Browne edged to Murali Vijay, standing next to him. It would unfold like that for Somerset. They were denied a story almost on every page. Comedian John Cleese and author Jeffrey Archer had been present throughout, these long-standing Somerset fans hoping on history. I read later of a journalist who travelled down as he had promised his father on his deathbed that he would be there when Somerset won the title.

Not that it was all romance of course. Had Essex lost 20 wickets on the final day then attention would have turned to the pitch preparation by the home side. Effectively, Somerset had been on a 12-month suspended sentence after being censured over their surface at the end of the previous season.

That period had run out a few weeks before this game so they were at liberty to create something more accommodating to their spin bowlers. In addition their groundsman was leaving for Hampshire at the end of the season.

As ever with cricket, there is so much subtlety here. Somerset would be have been docked points posthumously and so the ECB would have been faced with the prospect of taking away the county's first-ever title. This issue always bristles at Essex as the club were denied the title in 1989 after being docked 25 points due to a sub-standard pitch at Southchurch Park, Southend. In the end, Worcestershire would finish six points ahead. Having read around the issue, I have found few who defend the surface on its own merits, instead falling on the whataboutism of 'everyone was doing it' and 'we played on worse'.

For what it's worth, here is 'my truth' on the pitch issue:

- Essex would have also produced a favourable pitch had they been in the same predicament;

- in the end, these issues are very hard to judge as they are dependent on the bowlers'/batsmen's skill on the day. For example, van der Merwe's late hitting while Cook and Westley lasted over two hours in the first innings;

- but, given they needed to get 20 Essex wickets and the forecast was poor and unpredictable, it was indicative that Somerset chose to avoid batting last; and

- there have been points deductions in the past, but I believe Essex are the only county perceived to have lost a title on the back of one. Maybe we were owed one.

(The above was written in the days after the game at Somerset. They were my thoughts at the time. In fact, Somerset were penalised for the state of their pitch but only on 19 November, almost two months after Essex had lifted the trophy. They received a 24-point deduction which would come into effect in the 2020 season, half of which was suspended. While the rating of the pitch and the quality of its preparation were rightly questioned during the game, the timing of this decision was bizarre. We must assume that the disciplinary process would have been followed in the same manner whatever the result so, had Somerset won, their trophy would have been snatched back and handed to Essex six weeks later.)

There was a little Twitter patter afterwards about the merits of Essex winning the title. A lot of this was understandable heat-of-the-moment bitterness and rarely is a trophy won without someone somewhere wanting to smudge the shine before it is held aloft. In fairness, most independent observers had sympathy for Somerset but more admiration for Essex.

Yet again, for what it's worth, here's my 'truth' on the merits of the 2019 title winners.

- Essex lost only one game. It was the first, very badly, at Hampshire. After that, they showed a champion's grit. Somerset lost at all their main title rivals through the season – Yorkshire, Hampshire and Essex.

- The main Essex batsmen averaged considerably more than the main Somerset batsmen.

- The Essex key spinner was better than the Somerset key spinners.

- Essex won all their home games. Yes, they were on pitches favourable to their key weapon, Simon Harmer. But not so favourable as the Taunton pitch for the final game.

- The composition of the Essex team was largely eight or nine youth products plus Harmer, ten Doeschate and sometimes Siddle.

- Essex were hit by a key call-up, Peter Siddle, but England do not seem to fancy their other star performers.

- Essex played without an overseas player for the final three games and went with youngsters. They came off. Somerset signed Murali Vijay to boost their top-order batting in the final few games. He failed.

- Somerset were blown away at Hampshire in the penultimate game. Had they won, the Taunton wicket would have been very different in character.

Ultimately, all this does not matter. The table is the only arbiter. The romance of the Somerset story will only grow until they finally win the title and 2019 will be another chapter that only serves to build towards an emotional crescendo. When they win it, they will deserve it.

Ever since ten Doeschate was dismissed in the Essex first innings on the final day, I had been pacing my living room, occasionally shouting at the TV but mostly beating myself up for not being there. For someone who prizes sporting stories over everything else, I had denied myself the ultimate tale today. I'd gone into this season to write. Then it turned into therapy. There was almost a masochistic element in being prepared to slog it around the motorway to Edgbaston or the Ageas Bowl only to miss out on the trophy lift when it mattered. It was touching to see Alastair Cook, a highly decorated England captain, break off from a live TV interview by saying 'Sorry, I don't want to miss this' and then joining his champagne-soaked team-mates as they bobbed up and down for the pictures. The entire squad was there, even a cardboard cut-out of Peter Siddle, who had gone back to Australia.

We all thought the team had needed to be restrained in their celebrations after the Vitality Blast victory. On camera, ten Doeschate smiled: 'I don't think the team got the memo about that.' In interviews afterwards, the players said they celebrated for a couple of hours at Taunton then, from their social media posts, appeared to enjoy a raucous coach ride home. In an interview with Cricinfo, ten Doeschate said he woke up on Friday morning, still in his whites and nestled between Alastair Cook and Tom Westley in the coaches' room. Had this been Premier League football, the story of the celebrations would have overtaken that of the success. There would have been cameras at the ground the next day to chew over the events even though nothing had changed, headlines would be huge and phone-in callers would throw angry words towards presenters whose very aim was to elicit them. I loved the fact that county cricket allowed a team to be a team. They played together, won together and celebrated together.

Alastair Cook's interviews were illuminating. He talked about how his motivation on continuing his post-international career at Essex was 'Winning trophies with his mates' and he would stay on at least one more season as 'he promised Tendo'. Those words and the trophy lift were the last moments I caught before shooting out the door to a networking event for sports marketers in London. This had not been the sole reason for missing the denouement of the season but I had made a promise to attend. Quite why I felt any need to honour it, I just do not know.

I got there, talked meaningless tosh for a while and then slipped out at a time that could be considered to be rudely early. I was angry with myself and my mind was elsewhere. Taunton, to be precise. Essex had won the title. I should have been there. Idiot.

The next day, I sat down and summed up my moments of the season. That piece ends this chapter. On the Saturday, Essex pitched a tent on the outfield and invited members to come along to get pictures taken with the trophy. It was pleasing to see how many people turned up. I queued, had a shot with the trophies and took a last look around the ground. It was already bunkering down for winter; there was a large black tarpaulin across the square guarded by a signing saying 'Keep off the Outfield'.

Two weeks earlier in bright sunshine, ten Doeschate had walked off to a standing ovation after that century against Surrey. Just last Saturday, Essex had come back from the brink to win their first ever Twenty20 then they had added the jewel in the crown, the County Championship. It was the eighth in their history and exactly 40 years after their first.

While the 1979 season will always be etched in Essex CCC history as their greatest year, you could make a strong case for 2019 tucking in just behind. The county also collected two trophies in 1984, 1985 and 2008 while the 2017 fairy tale felt like a breakthrough of a new era. However, in 2019, Essex had been 50 points behind Somerset in the title race midway through the summer and looked adrift in their Twenty20 group after ten games. Fans love any sort of silverware but a comeback serves to multiply the drama. My club had provided two in a year.

But now it was all over. The finale had been wonderful then the curtain has crashed down in brutal, unforgiving fashion. The rather sombre scene across the outfield at Chelmsford matched my mood as I surveyed it for the last time in 2019.

This season had provided so much joy. Essex fans would do well to cherish it for years to come. Now we had to bunker down for winter and begin preparing for the following summer when domestic cricket may start to look very different.

The Moment

LET'S DRINK in the glory for a second. Before the glow of victory fades. Before life returns to normal. Before winter sets in. Because, right now, less than 24 hours after Essex lifted the County Championship title, there is only room for celebration. In fact, only the faint feelings of last night's triumphant alcohol can cloud my emotions.

You can keep the 'what ifs' of the Somerset pitch, the 'will hes' of close-season departures and the 'oh God… whens' of the Hundred. If sport is about moments then this is one. Right here, right now. Pause, capture its essence and put it in a safe place in your memory. Hopefully, it can keep you warm until April.

Even Sir Alastair Cook, the creator of some of the most important moments in English cricket history, wanted to savour the occasion at Taunton. That is why he excused himself from a live TV interview by saying 'Sorry, I don't want to miss this' before trotting over to join a bobbing, champagne-spraying gaggle of his team-mates.

As ever, the big moment comprised a series of small ones. This season, I went to a day of every away game bar

Headingley – I even turned up at Cambridge University in pre-season. I have no idea how many days at Chelmsford I saw. But it is certainly too many for my faltering career to comfortably cope with.

So here, with zero research and only my unreliable memory as a resource, are the mini-moments that made up the big one. Some are emotional, some statistical and some significant in the title race. But all, I believe, are meaningful.

Dan Lawrence and Ryan ten Doeschate batting v Surrey (A)

Look back at your social media. What were you posting after we got thrashed at Hampshire by an innings in the opening game of the season? I remember some people, let's call them 'knee-jerks', predicting relegation. Especially as, heaven help us, next up were the reigning champions at The Oval. The pressure was cranked up when Surrey posted a serious score and then Cook went early in the reply. But Lawrence and the skipper dug in and we returned with a creditable draw. A sign of the character to come.

Siddle and Sam Cook batting v Yorkshire (A)

Yorkshire were still in the title race in mid-season. We would have followed on and probably lost without these two tail-enders wagging furiously. Momentum was key to our title charge and this partnership maintained our form when it was still relatively fragile.

Harmer bowling v Hampshire (H)

Hampshire were contenders too. Harmer got a five-for and a seven-for. He had really hit his stride and Essex had worked out a method of winning at home. The spinner conjured up this sort of performance a few times and probably deserves more mentions in this list but this may be the best example of his craft.

A Cook batting and Beard bowling v Somerset (H)

Our knight in shining armour ground out 80 in the first innings and just short of 50 in the second. His aggregate was a huge contribution in the context of a low-scoring Chelmsford pitch this season, and he did it in a game that would open up the title race. Also, kudos should be thrown toward Aaron Beard, a rookie paceman who took seven wickets in the same game. His quality meant Somerset could not wait and feed on the third-string bowler. This sort of back-up was also important in our final games, when we operated without an overseas player.

Sam Cook bowling v Kent (A)

Mohammad Amir went back on his red-ball retirement to fill a Peter Siddle-shaped hole in the side at Kent. He played his part but Sam Cook, back from injury, raked over the Gardeners of England by taking 7-for-not-a-lot and skittled them for 40. This paceman stepped up this season.

Sam Cook and Porter bowling v Surrey (H)

These two ran through Surrey with five wickets apiece, including a vicious dual spell on the second morning when the visitors, smarting from criticism by their coach, had put in place a platform to build an imposing score. Lawrence and ten Doeschate got centuries and then Harmer did the rest. Meanwhile, Somerset were being gutted by Kyle Abbott at the Ageas Bowl.

And:

Wheater walking v Kent (A)

We were nine down in the first innings, well over a hundred short of Kent's score. The game was on the line and, with it, a significant advantage in the title race. Wheater was trying to negotiate the tail and another 30, 40 or 50 could be critical. When Kent appealed for a catch behind, the umpire hesitated but the Essex keeper did not. He walked. Chapeau, Adam.

There are loads more … Ravi's classy ton at Notts, Westley's big ton at Warwick, Cook's two time-consuming innings at Somerset, almost every time Harmer bowled at Chelmsford. This is not a researched list, it is just a reaction.

But they are a mosaic of memories that, fused together, produced that moment at Taunton late on Thursday evening.

I will try to savour them all before April.

The Winter (and discontent)

RYAN TEN Doeschate resigned the captaincy of Essex County Cricket Club on 21 January 2020. He had led the side in 58 first-class games over four seasons, winning 33 and losing only eight. During that time, the team's league positions had been first (with promotion from Division Two), first, third and first.

In his open letter on the club website, he wrote: 'I can't wait to join the troops, focus on my batting, and give the new captain all of my support in continuing to try to get the best out of our great club.' Later, in *The Cricketer* magazine, he would say the captaincy 'came at a really good time – it gave me a different focus' but that stepping away was 'not tough at all'.

For someone who had spent the last three years struggling for self-definition, the final quote was the most admirable of all. There would be 140 UK cricketers out of contract at the end of the 2020 season, and with county coffers already tight and an unbeknown economic calamity ahead, a high percentage would be cut adrift. From rookies to long-standing fans' favourites, everyone would be under scrutiny for their contribution. Many highly skilled players would never be professional cricketers ever again.

How would they cope? Firstly with not being a professional cricketer and secondly with having to find a job in what will be one of the most difficult employment markets in a century? What stories would they tell themselves? Would their anger go inwards towards themselves or randomly outwards towards their coach, partner, the system or whatever?

A large percentage of us grew up wanting to be professional athletes. The term 'failed cricketer' or 'failed footballer' seems puzzling as it tends to define those who were highly successful until the final hurdle or even had a few years in the pro game. I am a failed footballer and a failed cricketer too. I just happened to fall off the professional pathway when I missed out on representing my tiny district in west Essex as a ten-year-old. So the notion is not part of my psyche, although I still remember both the moment I was not selected for that side and the face of the PE teacher who left me out. The bastard.

In professional sport, the casualties are strewn across all age groups but especially those in the years immediately after retirement when those strong self-images are most in need of swift redefinition. They are now forever an 'ex-pro' and, for some, there is a hole where the defining part of them used to reside. Around 40 per cent of footballers go bankrupt because their spending patterns continue to match who they were, not who they are. Meanwhile, roughly a third are divorced within a couple of years. It is not just the UK – one in six NFL players go broke too. Newspapers run a healthy stream of stories about ex-professional athletes falling foul of alcohol, drugs, marital affairs or a lifestyle that bankrupts them. Many have been feted and supported since their teens and suddenly they have to change their personal image. The story on the way up tends to affect the story on the way down. 'If I hadn't seen such riches I could live with being poor' as the indie band James once sang.

Just before the 2020 season was scheduled to begin, *Wisden* named Simon Harmer as one of their Cricketers of the Year after 83 wickets in 2019. In the accompanying article, he conjured the quote of the season: 'Excuse my language, but some cricketers are kissed on the cock, and things come easy. I feel as though I am a late bloomer in life and in cricket: I have had to do things the hard way.'

Accepting an initial six-month contract worth £30,000 with Essex was a gamble given that his Kolpak status ended any international ambitions for South Africa. Since then, his dominance in county cricket has led to a clamour for an England call when he qualifies in 2021. Yet he still lived with insecurity as a mixture of red tape and Brexit had affected his qualification status. As a result, he could not buy a property in the UK and his girlfriend was unable to work.

'I'm very much a cricketing nomad,' he said. 'I pack up my life in boxes, store them and move on to the next place. It's extremely frustrating because, as much as I love Essex, I feel like I don't belong because I don't have somewhere to come back to.'

My trip through the 2019 season had been based on that very word, belonging. Having been emotionally displaced for years, one of the few places I still fitted was county cricket and specifically in the stands watching Essex CCC. Some might say I had moved into an age bracket when the cadence of the County Championship was more suited to my pace of life. But that was to miss the point. Like many in middle age, I had been struggling. Not for work, not for money, not for company, but for identity. Writing a book, another lifetime ambition, offered change, growth and served to organise the search for a year. But there was no guarantee of finding a solution and, anyway, The Hundred was still on the horizon.

Finally, the tournament seemed to be adding flesh to the bare bones that had satisfied no one during its conception. Not that it was straightforward. After the usual hype at the start of October, The Hundred Draft turned out to be dull, a little confusing and only added new areas of complaint. Northamptonshire batsman Josh Cobb was a Twenty20 specialist with the third-highest number of sixes in the Blast since 2018, yet he was overlooked. He suggested that not playing for one of the host counties was a factor. Generally, the non-hosting teams saw less of their players selected with Leicestershire's squad going undisturbed entirely. However, middle-ranking Sussex lost the most with 11 absences. Despite being one of the most eye-catching and expensive players on the list, West Indian batsman Chris Gayle was not selected but Kolpak players proved popular. In total, almost a third of the players chosen were not eligible for England.

A few days after the draft, ECB chairman Colin Graves and CEO Tom Harrison answered questions in front of the Culture, Media and Sport select committee in the House of Commons. Their performance drew criticism from the media and ridicule from traditional county fans but, barring waving a white flag and claiming 'mea culpa', that was always going to follow. In truth, their grilling fanned the final flames of real resistance. The Hundred was here and it was happening. The mood music was changing. Sentiment on social media had seemed aggressively opposed to the tournament since it was first mooted. Of course, the 'squeaky wheels' dominate on an echo chamber like Twitter so any support for a new tournament was always going to be softer and quieter. But, for much of the summer, it seemed tough to find a journalist or commentator not employed by one of the host broadcasters talking in favourable terms. That gradually changed. Likewise, many counties who had been loudly opposed lost their voice. Perhaps they were on board, perhaps they were tactically tight-lipped or perhaps there was a more malign meaning behind their silence. Certainly it seemed that fatigue had set in and other plates were moving into position.

It was noticeable that, by this time, the BBC Sport website had already set up a prominent section for The Hundred yet the corporation had deemed the County Championship not worthy of the merest mention in 2017 on its flagship annual event, *Sports Personality of the Year* (SPOTY). The ECB could argue that was some of the cut-through their deal had bought and, with the licence fee under more scrutiny than ever before, the BBC would contend they needed to develop and effectively promote their own products.

However, when as happened in 2018, that night's SPOTY occupies five of the top six stories on the BBC website on the afternoon in which Liverpool have just beaten Manchester United to go top of the Premier League, you start to feel the pure editorial judgement is starting to be tainted by other agendas. Fans can be biased, players can be biased, even newspapers can be biased but one always expects more of the BBC and the governing body of a sport. That is why every nuance of political reporter Laura Kuenssberg was examined during the General Election coverage and the motives of those imposing The Hundred were under scrutiny when for so long they had failed to explain their reasoning.

Like English domestic cricket, trustworthy media needs money to stay relevant. Quality journalism that educates, informs and entertains sucks up resources. You need even deeper pockets for the investigative, analytical and challenging work that tends to make a difference to society. In contrast, click-bait crap is made to monetise. Newspapers were the first media to suffer after the first internet revolution. The local level was hit hardest with almost 200 titles disappearing after 2005, including my old stomping ground at the *Aldershot News*. A study in 2016 found towns that lost their paper suffered a 'deficit of democracy', citing the example of the 71 lives lost in the fire at Grenfell Tower. A blog had foreseen the danger in the west London block of flats but the local paper had closed, leaving a lone reporter covering the patch from a hub in Surrey. Local newspapers, physical or digital, are vital to a community, even if they are not financially viable. So, it is the BBC who are stepping into the breach with their Local Democracy Reporter scheme. In 2019, they were paying the salaries of 150 journalists across the UK who would share their output with commercial outlets. They were even looking for private companies to assist, mirroring the way US philanthropists fund not-for-profit companies to create public interest journalism.

Having travelled around the circuit in 2019, there seems to be no rationale for 18 teams to be playing County Championship cricket either. The England Test team could be serviced by a dozen just as well. But like so many, I want it to exist as a fully fledged national competition. It is not essential for democracy like the loss of local newspapers but there would be a 'deficit of soul' within the country without it. Clearly, there are 'remote fans' in the woodwork. That is why they jumped on Twenty20 when it emerged and made the effort to attend key Championship games at the end of recent seasons. Sports teams are big brands but not necessarily big business. There will be out-of-town supermarkets in the UK whose turnover is greater than that of their nearest Premier League club. However, no one arrives at Tesco an hour before the action starts or sings of their devotion and previous successful shopping trips as they traverse the aisles. Sport has always encouraged a special and quite peculiar devotion.

Many football teams talk of being more than a club, but fail to deliver. In reality, short-term money is spent on manufacturing short-term success. Fans enfranchise this thinking but then pay for it, fiscally and emotionally, through consistent booms and busts. Could cricket be different? Could a less demanding fanbase accept a different way of doing business, given that cold, hard economics could not sustain the sport in its longest domestic form?

The Guardian newspaper did this in 2014. Faced with losses, a change in the advertising market and the increasing power of social media giants, they launched a membership scheme. In order to uphold their principle of keeping online content free, they supplemented their usual revenue streams with a tiered offering based on building a community. There were events and clubs; you could even learn with *The Guardian*. If you did not want to be tied in, you could make a straight contribution. In 2018, they boasted 570,000 regular-paying 'supporters' and 375,000 one-off 'donators'. By 2019, they were hoping to bring in 30 per cent of their revenue this way. For good or bad, the '*Guardian* reader' is a stereotype in the UK and this group had clearly heard the call. If you wanted the newspaper to exist in its current form then you had to be prepared to chip in – the company just had to provide a value proposition to entice you.

This is the seam of ideas that county cricket has to mine now. It has got to behave in a different way and offer a different vision, emphasising its social role just as much as its sporting importance. In 2019, I attended many Championship games where the crowd was over 2,000. But for each one, I saw a day among 500 or so fellow fans. Still, the four-day game has been remarkably resilient and there is certainly enough life left to justify its continued existence. But there needs to be a re-evaluation if it wants to grow and develop, not just survive. Twenty20 seems to be the dominant format everywhere and, while Test matches retain relevance in the UK, there is concern about their long-term global appeal and the television rights fees they can command. If that weakens, the quid-pro-quo arrangement between the national team and the County Championship could crumble. This fear led to The Hundred in the first place. It was right to do something, just not that. I do not profess to have the answer, I am merely proposing a different way to pose the question, one based on what cricket can mean, not what it can make.

Still, as I had found out over the past few years, changing one 50-year-old person is hard enough. Let alone 18 counties, millions of fans and almost 150 years of history.

So, we all prepared for the new campaign. That meant pre-ordering the *Wisden Cricketers' Almanack*, whose yellow cover remains the surest sign of summer. I also put *The Cricketer*'s county wall planner up in my office.

The 2020 domestic season had been discussed for five years, garnering more attention than any in living memory. Finally, it was here.

And then it wasn't.

Conclusion
(and then the world changed)

PERHAPS IT was inevitable that a book about coping with change would have to make drastic alterations to its conclusion. The plan had been to arrive nice and early at Chelmsford on 19 April for the opening game of the 2020 County Championship season, settle down in front of the pavilion and watch Essex reach 232/2 against Yorkshire at the end of the first day's play. In the intervals, I'd pull out my laptop and, flush with the brio of a new campaign, opine one last time on the injustice of everything that lay ahead. This volume would then thump on to the desk of sports editors around the UK just as The Hundred spewed into life as if to say 'ha, take that'.

It even occurred to tie up everything in a nice Dickensian bow. I would pick up my quill one last time and write: 'Thank you, dear reader, for journeying with me on this search for meaning in county cricket. While the game seemed to be cowering under a number of question marks, at least I had found my answer in writing about the search for its future. Returning to my first love had been cleansing, refreshing and fortifying in equal measure.' Finally, with renewed assurance and staggering self-importance, I would howl 'self-criticism be damned, henceforth I would be a sportswriter once more'. Cue the swirling smoke, cue a crescendo of strings, cue closing titles.

However, the Coronavirus crisis that swept the world in the second quarter of 2020 would change everything. When lives are being lost, sport suddenly reverts to its proper place as a minor diversion. Likewise, one's personal concerns of identity, meaning and workplace fulfilment look like mere bleating. Yet, that should not delegitimise what has gone before. It should be understood within its proper context. Hence the previous chapters remain, in their essence, untouched. Everyone has altered their views in fundamental ways as a result of COVID-19. Not least our politicians, many of whom were urging us to clap support for the NHS despite having left the institution cruelly underfunded in previous decades and, in some circumstances, actively voted against pay raises for those who were now risking their lives to keep the population safe.

In the relatively trivial world of English cricket, ECB chief executive Tom Harrison immediately talked of rewarding the 'core audience' once the lockdown had been lifted. This was the very group which, by word and deed, had felt systematically disenfranchised by the manner of The Hundred's introduction. While their five-year plan called 'Inspiring Generations' included positive planks such as Dynamos cricket for eight- to 11-year-olds and the South Asian Action Plan, it had neglected to nurture the very people who stimulate and enthuse the young –

their parents and grandparents. 'Because my dad does' is a standard answer as to why anyone takes up a sport or supports a team. The previous 12 months had done much to shake the faith of those who had a long-standing love of the sport for those who ran it.

Some respect was clawed back by the English cricket authorities response to the crisis. Perhaps it was the perilous nature of county finances, perhaps it was previous battles, perhaps it was sound leadership, but the game appeared relatively united. Almost immediately, professional cricket was put on hold until 28 May and various scenarios were created depending on the eventual lifting of the lockdown. Cancelling the entire season would cost the game an estimated £300m and potentially push a number of counties off the ledge on which they had been tottering for years. Everyone knew cold hard cash must be the priority now. A few argued for some sort of four-day tournament if there was time at the end of the season. However, the first seven Championship rounds had been scrubbed off the fixture list due to the initial cessation and a shortened version seemed meaningless both in a financial and sporting sense. Tellingly, almost no one spoke up for the 50-over competition and this revelation may mean it is one of the longer-term casualties of the Coronavirus. If there was a competitive domestic cricket season, the consensus was it must consist of The Hundred and/or the T20 Blast. We would all have to get behind it, no matter which tournament was prioritised. In the end, the Blast was the clear choice. This was entirely the wrong time to launch a new competition like The Hundred and, crucially, there seemed to be latitude from the broadcasters. Meanwhile, the Blast would raise the most gate revenue, was the easiest to accommodate and had an established audience. According to two lines down page in the *Daily Mail*, pre-sale tickets for the Blast had 'surged' this year, even in comparison to 2019 record figures. The Hundred's PR machine had made much of 100,000 sales 'inside the first 24 hours of widespread availability' but those tickets were much cheaper and, again, fans had cause to question the claim.

All this nit-picking may sound unnecessary in the wake of the global pandemic that was set to contract the British economy by up to a third and plunge the world into recession. However, in addition to a desire to spin the positive to within an inch of untruth, the modern approach to any sort of crisis is to 'move on' as quickly as possible. In 2019, the public got bored of the long battle over Brexit and just wanted closure. The general attitude towards The Hundred had moved in a similar direction during the winter. Now we had reached 2020 everyone needed to give it a chance, right? The problem was that serious question marks still lay at the heart of the thought process, implementation and communication of both. The key difference was the public had voted for Brexit whereas The Hundred was pushed forward by the powers-that-be. It was clear that both were going to be engineered by the victors so they could be painted as successful. The question was for whom?

Whatever happens, one hopes that the UK government's handling of the Coronavirus comes under serious scrutiny. It is not about finding fault but holding those in power to constructive examination. Nothing will ever get better unless we try to actively learn from our mistakes. In the midst of this period, there was a feeling that we could build a better world from the wreckage of the old. The same was true in the most important of those unimportant things – sport. The response by the ECB looked clear and relatively commanding, certainly in comparison to football. Over £60m was put towards a rescue package, £40m as a stimulus for the counties and clubs, £20m in grants and interest-free loans for the recreational game. The England players contributed £500,000 as a donation to the grassroots game, ECB executive staff agreed to a short-term pay reduction of 20 per cent while Harrison voluntarily went five per cent higher than that. At the start of April, Yorkshire CCC became the first elite sports team in the UK to furlough its players. Gradually, most counties took up the government's job retention scheme whereby 80 per cent of monthly wages were covered up to £2,500. On 8 April, Essex announced their players would join the club's general staff on this arrangement.

So, having spent 6 April 2019 at the Ageas Bowl attempting to stop Hampshire reaching 500 in the opening game of the season, Simon Harmer and Tom Westley spent 6 April 2020 helping to prepare 1,000 hot meals for NHS staff across 13 hospitals in Essex and London. The club website showed a group of six players spooning dishes from giant vats into plastic tubs then lifting crates into the backs of vans. The public relations around cricket was truly uplifting at this time. Essex players phoned members to see how they were coping with the isolation. The emphasis was on those of pensionable age as more than 20 per cent of the 5,000 Essex members were over 70 years old and considered 'high risk'. However, children got calls too. Cricket's social media became highly creative if slightly eccentric with many individuals posting on general view those moments that would usually be reserved for an idle daydream in front of the bathroom mirror. England bowler Mark Wood showed the world a dance routine while BBC London commentator Mark Church produced a series of delightful reflections on key moments in cricket history with members of his family as summarisers. The Essex squad even sang to raise funds for the NHS. On what would have been the opening day of the season, fans and players alike used the #CountyChampAtHome hashtag to post videos of them batting in the back garden. There were many emotional tributes from those who still considered this to be a quasi-holy day.

During the afternoon of 30 April, the ECB finally announced that The Hundred would be postponed until the following year. The lockdown had been extended and, at this point, it seemed that, if there was to be any cricket that summer, it would be played behind closed doors. The news had been expected to drop the previous Friday. When it did not, there was a ripple of media conjecture that the governing body were rethinking the entire competition. In fact, the ECB would double down with Harrison telling *The Guardian*: 'I don't think [this crisis] in any way dilutes the case for The Hundred, it absolutely accelerates it and makes it something cricket needs to get behind. I am absolutely committed [to The Hundred], as I think the whole game is. The first-class counties understand its importance to the future of the game and how it will help us achieve stability for everything the game has cared about for hundreds of years. That's super-important to us.'

Columnist Vic Marks was not the first to compare his boldness to US president Donald Trump. The ex-Somerset spinner also suggested the approach was reminiscent of his former team-mate Ian Botham, the type of bowler who would be hit for successive fours and then request another slip. In reality, there was no certainty right now. My year-long odyssey around the County Championship had been prompted by the fear that this new competition would eventually spell the end of clubs like Essex. All the while, I was searching for personal re-invention. As ever, your worries are not what should be really troubling you. The greater threat to the Championship was invisible and unforeseen. One report predicted that COVID-19 could send 14 of the 18 county clubs out of business. The likes of Warwickshire earned 84 per cent of their revenue on matchdays, and Surrey took in 73 per cent that way. Gaping holes had opened up in balance sheets among many organisations already saddled with debt. Like most businesses in the country, they were going to have to ask for central support like never before. That meant a major mental shift for many traditional fans. Suddenly the bad guys were not the bad guys anymore; in fact, we all had to believe they were the good guys now. Talk about a plot twist. Summing up the mood, the leading pressure group Oppose The Hundred tweeted: 'The delay of The Hundred is not a cause for celebration when the entire sport is under threat and we may see no cricket for some time. People's lives are at risk and cricket is in trouble. I wish everyone at ECB Cricket every success in steering cricket through this crisis.' Incredibly, some fans gave them flak for it.

For all the criticism they have garnered during the development of The Hundred, the governing body were really guilty of doing the wrong thing, the wrong way for the right reasons. In this book, I have not tried to hide the problems in English domestic cricket. Much of what I have presented should support the need for change – some might even use it to back The Hundred. But my role was not to take a stance and then construct an argument for it. I was considering one season, following my team in search of cricket's soul and personal salvation. The former was obvious, even if you had to go to Southampton on a bleak morning in April to reveal it. The latter remains elusive but writing this book has helped. Thank you for reading it.

Change is always inevitable but, in the post-COVID-19 world, there will be no luxury of prevarication. Who knows what we might have to accept? If familiar High Street stores and long-established, previously profitable family businesses go under then can loss-making counties reasonably expect to go on? Once it has all played out maybe there will be mergers, maybe there will be liquidations or maybe The Hundred will be all we have.

I truly hope that the beauty of county cricket can survive this crisis, not in the wounded way it has traipsed through the last few decades but as something stronger. A vibrant mix of the long- and short-form game, with deep roots in its communities and strength at all levels of participation. But above all, a sport that stands for something, in possession of true meaning and values, existing as something more than a product to be monetised. The opportunity is there, ironically more than any of us thought at the start of 2020.

Should we not grasp it, memories of 2019, a season that saw a World Cup, an Ashes series and, most gloriously for me, a County Championship victory, may be all we have in summers to come.

A Message from Opening Up

A CHARITY promoting mental well-being and suicide prevention through cricket.

To aid understanding of what works best for your mental health there are some excellent resources available online. The NHS 'Every Mind Matters' (https://www. nhs.uk/oneyou/every-mind-matters) site gives you the opportunity to create your own plan to look after your mind, tailored to your particular preferences. Alongside this, apps such as Headspace and Smiling Mind provide a platform to practise mindfulness, a technique with a string of benefits to mental health. People find this can help switch off and deal with change in life amongst many other things.

Physical exercise provides benefits to mental wellbeing and there's plenty on offer through groups like Move It or Lose It (https://www.moveitorloseit.co.uk/) who provide classes for people who may not be already active and wish to be.

Many county boards have an offer for walking cricket if you still fancy being involved in the sport but have lapsed from the regular game.

A further source of good mental wellbeing can be found through volunteering. If you find yourself with more time and a willingness to help others then you can find options here (https://www.gov.uk/government/get-involved/take-part/volunteer) or seek opportunities within your local cricket club.

Select Bibliography

Books

Lemmon D., *Summer of Success: The Triumph of Essex County Cricket Club in 1979* (London: Pelham Books 1980)

Lemmon D., Marshall M., *Essex County Cricket Club: The Official History* (London: Kingswood Press 1987)

Hamilton D., *A Last Summer* (London: Quercus, 2010)

McDonald B., *Invisible Ink: A Practical Guide to Building Stories that Resonate* (USA: Talking Drum 2017)

Wisden Cricketers' Almanack, various years

Podcasts

Wisden Cricket Monthly

The Tim Ferriss Show

Don't Tell Me The Score, BBC

Film Stories with Simon Brew

The Broken Wicket, TBW Media

All The Overs – Essex Cricket Podcast

98 Not Out – Phoenix FM

Kermode and Mayo

Magazines
The Cricketer
Wisden Cricket Monthly
County Cricket Matters

Websites
Cricinfo
BBC Sport
Daily Telegraph
The Times
The Guardian
Daily Mail
Essex CCC
Opening Up